onkeys

Led By Donkeys

Projection on the
Houses of Parliament,
2 April 2024, 9:30pm.

Adventures in
Art, Activism and
Accountability

Led
By
Donkeys

With 395 illustrations

Contents

Introduction

For a while we were anonymous.

After putting our kids to bed we'd go out late at night to paste up giant posters in towns and cities across Britain – an effort to expose the ineptitude and hypocrisy of Britain's governing class – and nobody knew who we were. But as public support for the project grew and hostile media outlets speculated about our identities, we took the decision to out ourselves.

There's only so long you can run an accountability project that's not fully accountable.

In retrospect, it was the moment that Led By Donkeys took off. We never wanted to make it about us, hoping instead that the work would speak for itself. Over the following months and years the project evolved into a guerrilla journalism operation that merges deeply-sourced research with creativity and direct action to fight populist politics and petty nationalism.

But accountability is still at the core of it all. We're trying, in our own small way, to hold powerful people responsible for what they've said and done, to chip away at the impunity so many of them enjoy in an age of hyper-partisan media. Politicians and influential commentators, not least those on the populist right, can nowadays pursue wildly successful careers by preaching nonsense, lies and half-truths to the supporters with whom they share a bubble. It's our job to prick it.

We're fortunate that there are large numbers of people prepared to back that effort – be it by sharing our interventions online, collaborating with us or donating to the project. Led By Donkeys has a policy of only accepting smaller donations so we're not compromised by dependence on any single individual. Apart from our original guerrilla poster campaign, none of the interventions featured here would have been possible without the backing of many thousands of supporters.

The objective is to build interventions that get large numbers of people talking and it's not uncommon for one of them to be seen by more people than watch the evening news on TV. Some of our films have been among the most viewed in the world that day on social media, beaten only by K-pop bands we've never heard of. Occasionally our output makes us laugh, but humour is just a tactic. We're trying to land fact-based campaigns with enough emotional resonance to dilute the tide of chauvinism and misinformation in which our political culture has been mired since 2016.

That might mean a collaboration with the team behind the TV drama *Line of Duty* (page 115) or it could be a projection on Buckingham Palace (page 34). Whatever it is we're doing, we try to hold on to the sentiment that propelled us up ladders with buckets of wallpaper paste back in 2019. If we have a decent idea we'll do it. It might be close to impossible, but if there's even a chance of pulling it off then we'll usually give it a go. This was the ethos that saw us install the half-kilometre-long National Covid Memorial Wall opposite Parliament (page 88), and to take over the White Cliffs of Dover with the story of a refugee's journey to Britain (page 74).

But the world doesn't end at Dover. We're internationalists (Nigel Farage would call us 'globalists') who see the struggle against ethnic-jingoism as universal. Thus, these pages also include interventions on the wars in Ukraine (page 170) and Gaza (page 210).

Does any of this make a difference? We think so. We hope so. There's a battle underway to shape the myths this country tells itself about itself, and this is our contribution to that story war. The preaching of British exceptionalism by Johnson, Farage and their fellow travellers has been a curse that has doomed us, paradoxically, to decline. The enemy was never asylum seekers, Brussels bureaucrats or foreign courts. It was and is corruption, incompetence, sophistry and nationalism here at home.

Oliver Knowles

Will Rose

James Sadri

Ben Stewart

Guerrilla Billboards

MULTIPLE LOCATIONS / UK

The start of the project. As mayhem enveloped Westminster and the supposed sunlit uplands of Brexit receded into a mist of intra-party rancour, we resolved to unearth some of the predictions and promises made by leading politicians. The first Led By Donkeys intervention, two weeks into 2019, was to print out David Cameron's infamous tweet predicting 'chaos with Ed Miliband' and paste it up on a busy intersection in north London. This meant learning how to install a guerrilla billboard – a discipline, we discovered, that's more challenging than it first appears.

The Cameron poster was, to our surprise, an online phenomenon and we were soon out at night at regular intervals on a mission to expose more incompetence and political hypocrisy. Fox and Raab statements were posted in Dover, Johnson in Birmingham. Some were tweets, others were quotes designed as tweets. Within a fortnight the public was donating money so the posters could be installed legitimately across the nation. One Farage poster was pasted above an abandoned SUV in Sunderland.

Dr Liam Fox MP ✓
@LiamFox

The Free Trade Agreement that we will do with the European Union should be one of the easiest in human history.

12:24 pm - 20 Jul 2017

112 Retweets 248 Likes

#LedByDonkeys @ByDonkeys

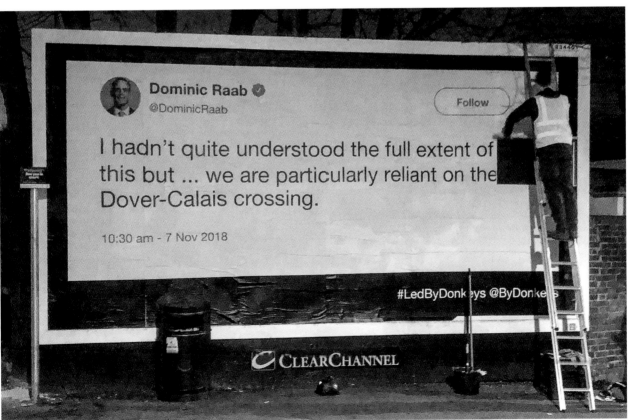

Dominic Raab ✓
@DominicRaab

I hadn't quite understood the full extent of this but ... we are particularly reliant on the Dover-Calais crossing.

10:30 am - 7 Nov 2018

#LedByDonkeys @ByDonkeys

CLEARCHANNEL

Boris Johnson ✔
@BorisJohnson

Fuck business.

12:30 pm - 22 Jun 2018

Foll

#LedByDonk

Nigel Farage ✓
@Nigel_Farage

If Brexit is a disaster,
abroad, I'll go and liv

27 Mar 2017

He didn't tweet it, he actually **said** it!
On his LBC radio show. **What changed?**

The March to Leave

SUNDERLAND TO LONDON / UK

Nigel Farage declared Brexit was being thwarted and announced he would lead an army of hundreds of patriots on a march from Sunderland to Parliament Square (the concept was a distasteful nod to the Jarrow March). We knew Farage's protest would garner massive media attention on its first day, but what would happen after that? How many supporters would be in for the long haul and would Farage stick around?

We joined on day one (that's one of us in Farage's tweet, on the left holding up a phone camera) with an ad van that broadcast a film exposing his hypocrisy. He was forced to walk past the van and, on one occasion, to endure it being parked in the pub car park where he and his crew were taking a lunch break. Later, as he stood atop his battlebus, the van slid into place below him.

As predicted, Farage soon bailed on the march and returned to London. We stuck with it, using a drone to record its diminishing attendance numbers and pasting a poster along the route.

Nigel Farage ✔
@Nigel_Farage

The #MarchToLeave has begun!

11:59 am · 16 Mar 2019

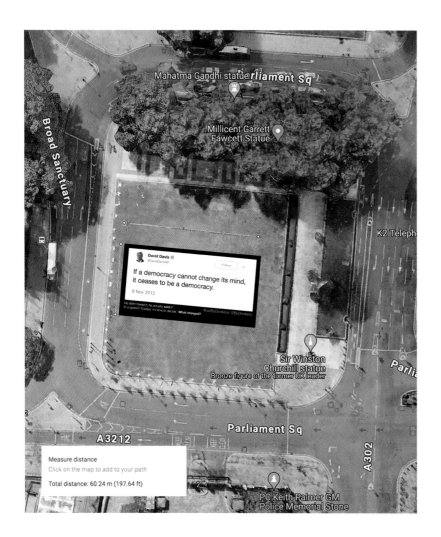

Democracy Crowd Banner

PARLIAMENT SQUARE, LONDON / UK

Hundreds of thousands were expected to march in London in support of a second referendum on Brexit and the organisers asked us if we could contribute something to the day. Our idea was inspired by football supporters who print massive crowd banners that are passed over heads at matches. Consulting Google Earth we worked out our banner could be 40m x 20m so we printed an 800m² rendition of a David Davis quote. On a signal from the stage we lifted the corners and ran it over the heads of the crowd in Parliament Square before they took over.

Breaking Point

SMITH SQUARE, LONDON / UK

UKIP's original Breaking Point poster was xenophobic and dangerous propaganda. Farage launched it in June 2016. Hours later MP Jo Cox was murdered by a white supremacist.

At the point of peak Brexit chaos we identified the people who were the real threat to our country (not refugees) and after a gargantuan Photoshop effort we had a re-worked version of the poster. We then tracked down the exact same ad van Farage used in 2016 to launch the original, put our version on the side and took it to Smith Square, where Farage's poster had been unveiled.

1. Boris Johnson	10. David Davis	19. Digby Jones	28. Michael Fabricant
2. Dominic Raab	11. Jeremy Hunt	20. Michael Gove	29. Suella Braverman
3. Chris Grayling	12. Theresa May	21. Paul Dacre	30. Andrew Bridgen
4. Jacob Rees-Mogg	13. Nigel Farage	22. Charles Moore	31. Patrick Minford
5. Iain Duncan Smith	14. Nadine Dorries	23. Kate Hoey	32. Graham Stringer
6. Arron Banks	15. John Redwood	24. Nick Timothy	33. Nigel Lawson
7. Andrea Leadsom	16. Daniel Kawczynski	25. Mark Francois	34. Sir William Cash
8. Liam Fox	17. Owen Paterson	26. Penny Mordaunt	35. Dominic Cummings
9. Rupert Murdoch	18. Daniel Hannan	27. Gisela Stuart	36. Esther McVey

37. Viscount Ridley
38. Peter Lilley
39. Peter Bone
40. Crispin Blunt
41. Andy Wigmore
42. John Whittingdale
43. Darren Grimes
44. Bernard Jenkin
45. Theresa Villiers

46. Steve Hilton
47. Marcus Fysh
48. Zac Goldsmith
49. Priti Patel
50. Philip Davies
51. Steve Baker
52. Steve Bannon
53. Vladimir Putin
54. Bernie Ecclestone

55. Donald Trump
56. Nigel Dodds
57. Sammy Wilson
58. Andrew Rosindell
59. Matthew Elliot
60. Andrea Jenkyns
61. Anne-Marie Trevelyan
62. Douglas Carswell
63. Arlene Foster

64. Ben Bradley
65. Tim Martin
66. David Cameron
67. Geert Wilders
68. Katie Hopkins
69. James Dyson
70. Seumas Milne
71. Gareth Snell
72. Caroline Flint

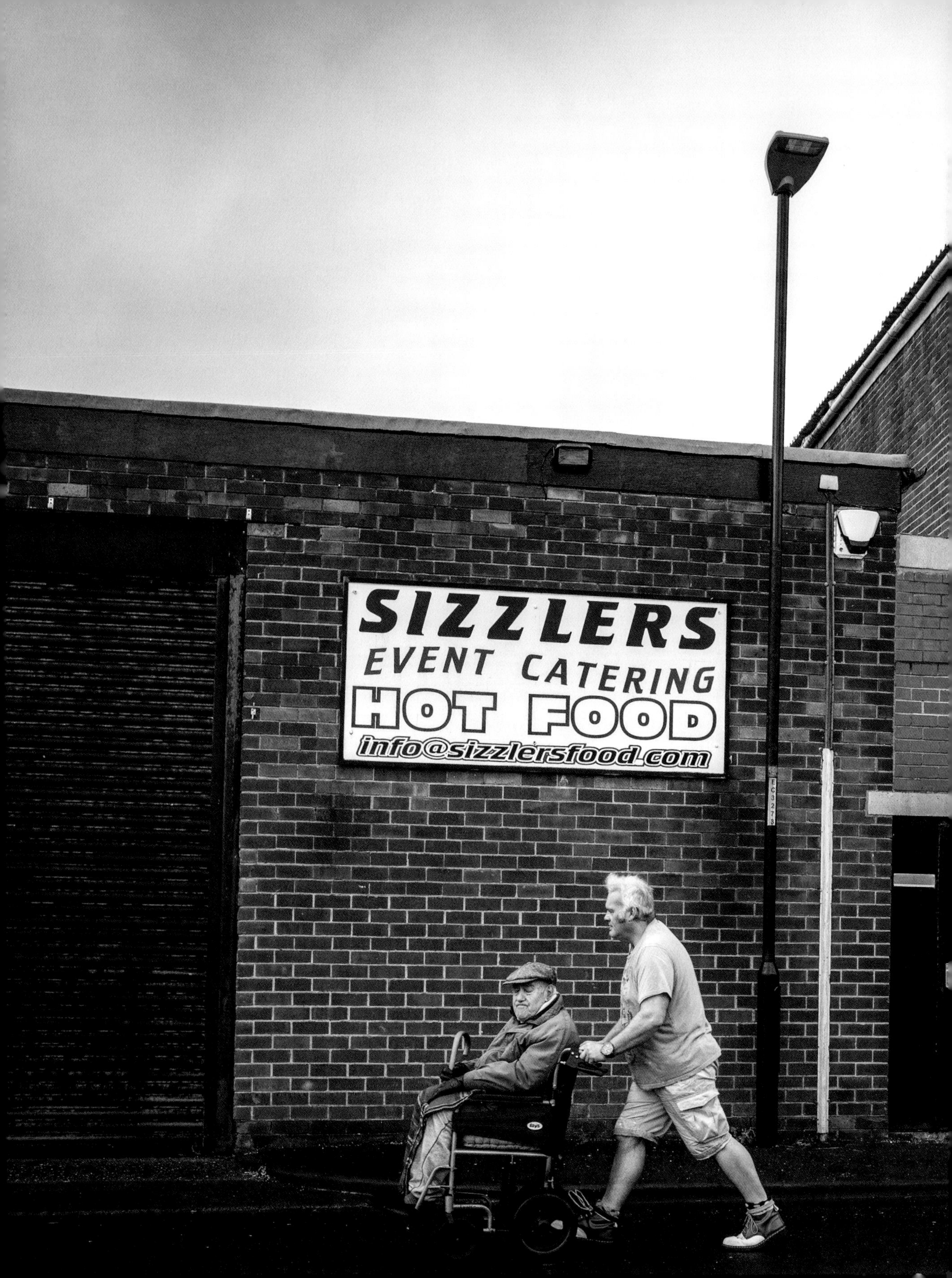
SIZZLERS
EVENT CATERING
HOT FOOD
info@sizzlersfood.com

THE TORIES ARE LYING

They are a danger to our NHS.
A&E waiting lists are at their worst ever level.

Printed by Augustus Martin 8-18 St.Andrews Way, Bromley-By-Bow, London E3 3PB, Augustus Martin Ltd does not endorse the content matter of this poster.
Promoted by Will Rose on behalf of Led By Donkeys, both of 71-75 Shelton Street, London, United Kingdom, WC2H 9JQ.

Led ByDonkeys

ClearChannel

Tel/Fax:0191-5147444 **STADIUM** E.stadiumtradeframes@hotmail.co.uk
TRADE FRAMES LTD
MANUFACTURERS OF:
REHAU U.P.V.C WINDOWS & DOORS

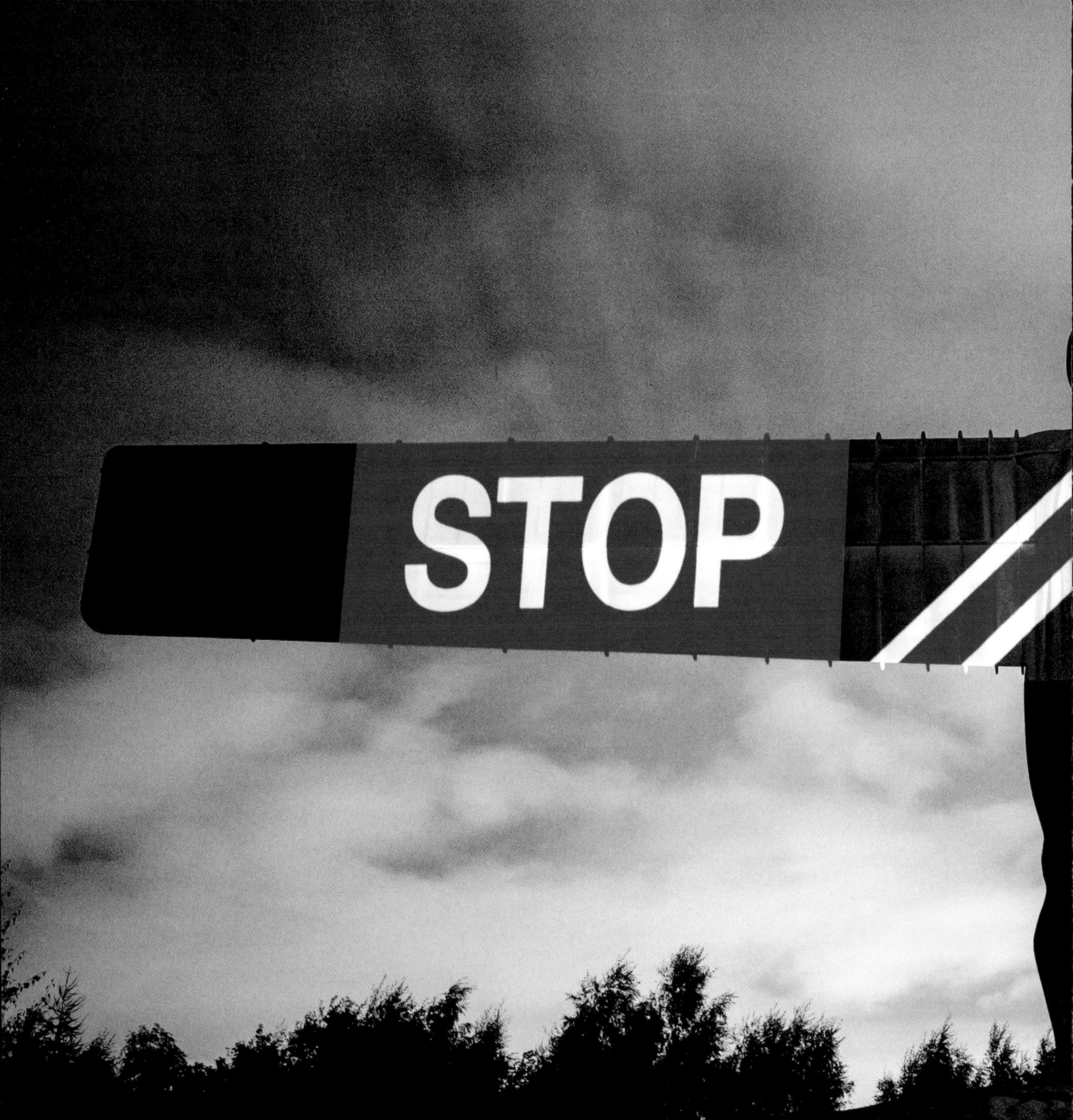
STOP

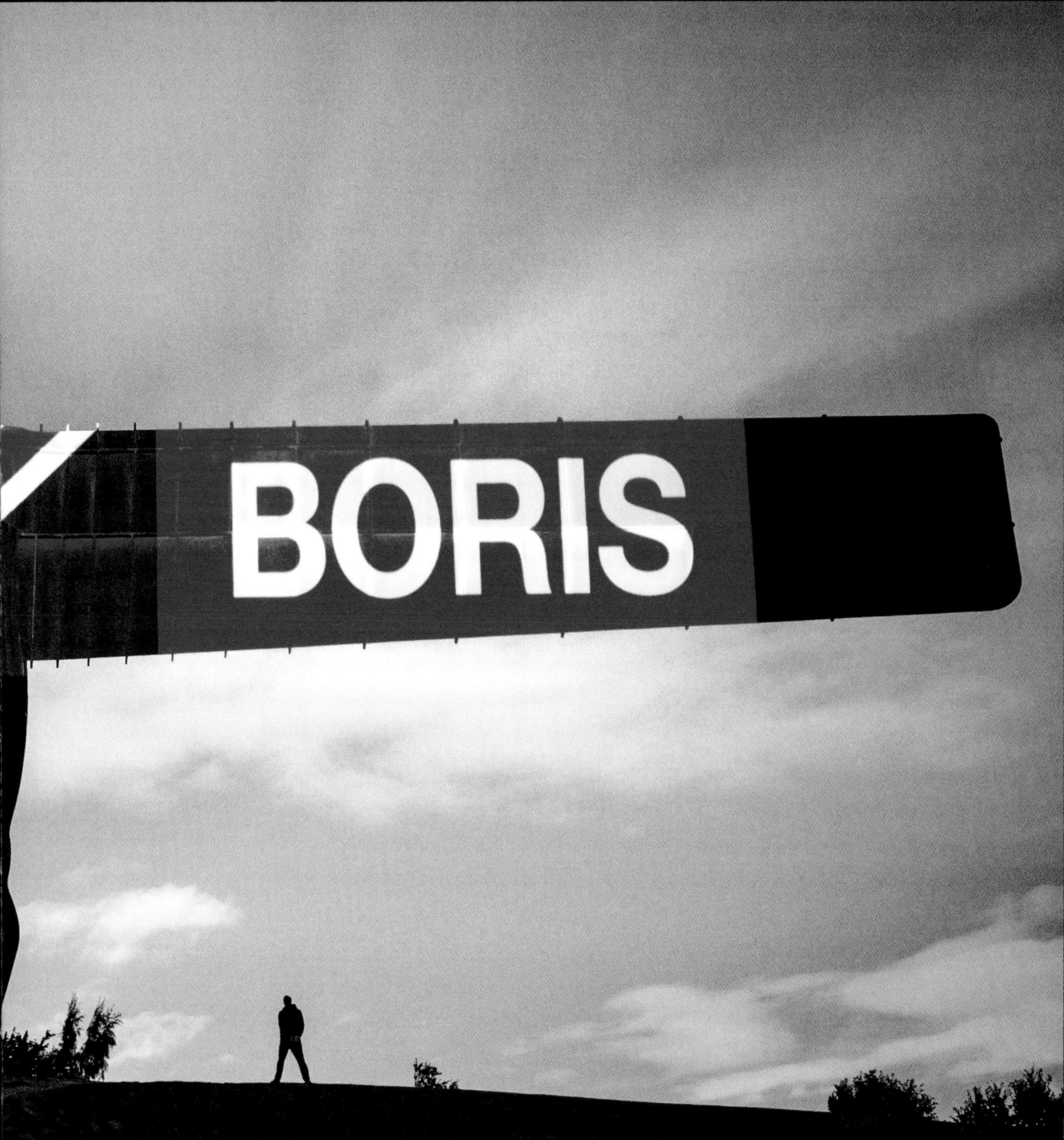
BORIS

The Tories Are Lying

SUNDERLAND, TYNE AND WEAR / UK

Stop Boris

ANGEL OF THE NORTH, GATESHEAD / UK

Trump's State Visit

LONDON / UK

In June Britain was afforded the pleasure of a state visit by
US President Donald Trump. Judging from his public statements
Mr Trump was labouring under the misapprehension that he was
popular in the UK. We took the projector to the Tower of London to
disabuse him of that notion before moving on to the National Gallery.
The intervention was covered on US TV channels.

Your Majesty

BUCKINGHAM PALACE, LONDON / UK

It was the first day of Boris Johnson's premiership, hours before
his scheduled trip to the Palace to accept an invitation from the
Queen to form a government. He was a serial liar, but few were
saying it publicly. As the projector blinked into life, an electrical
storm split the sky above our heads (see page 34).

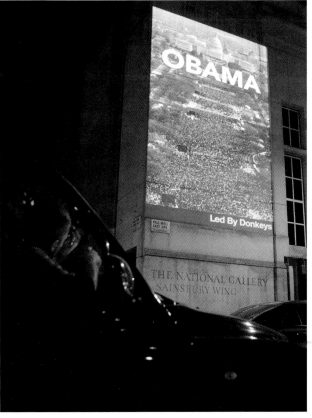

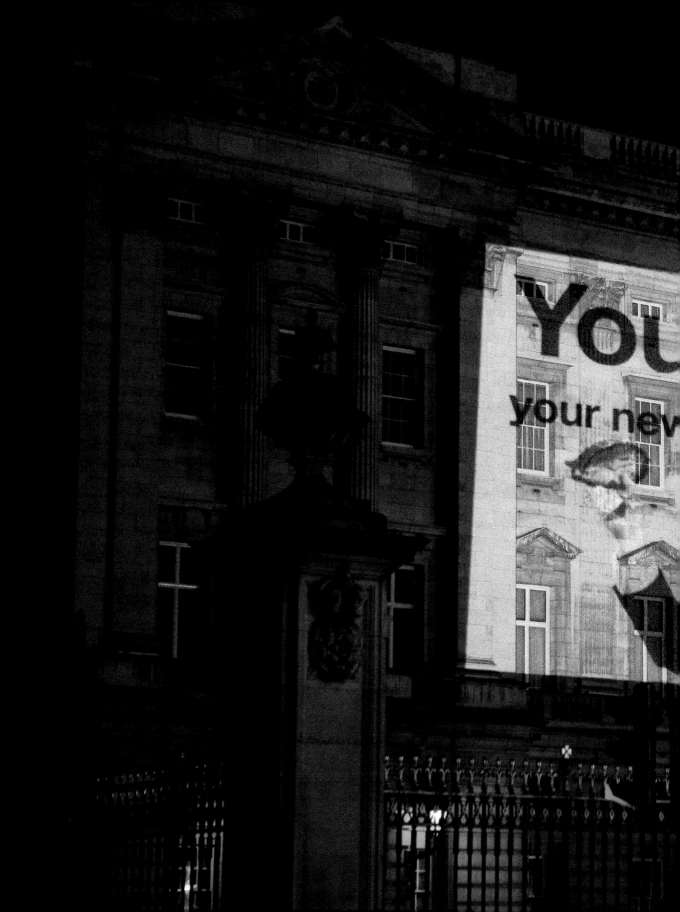

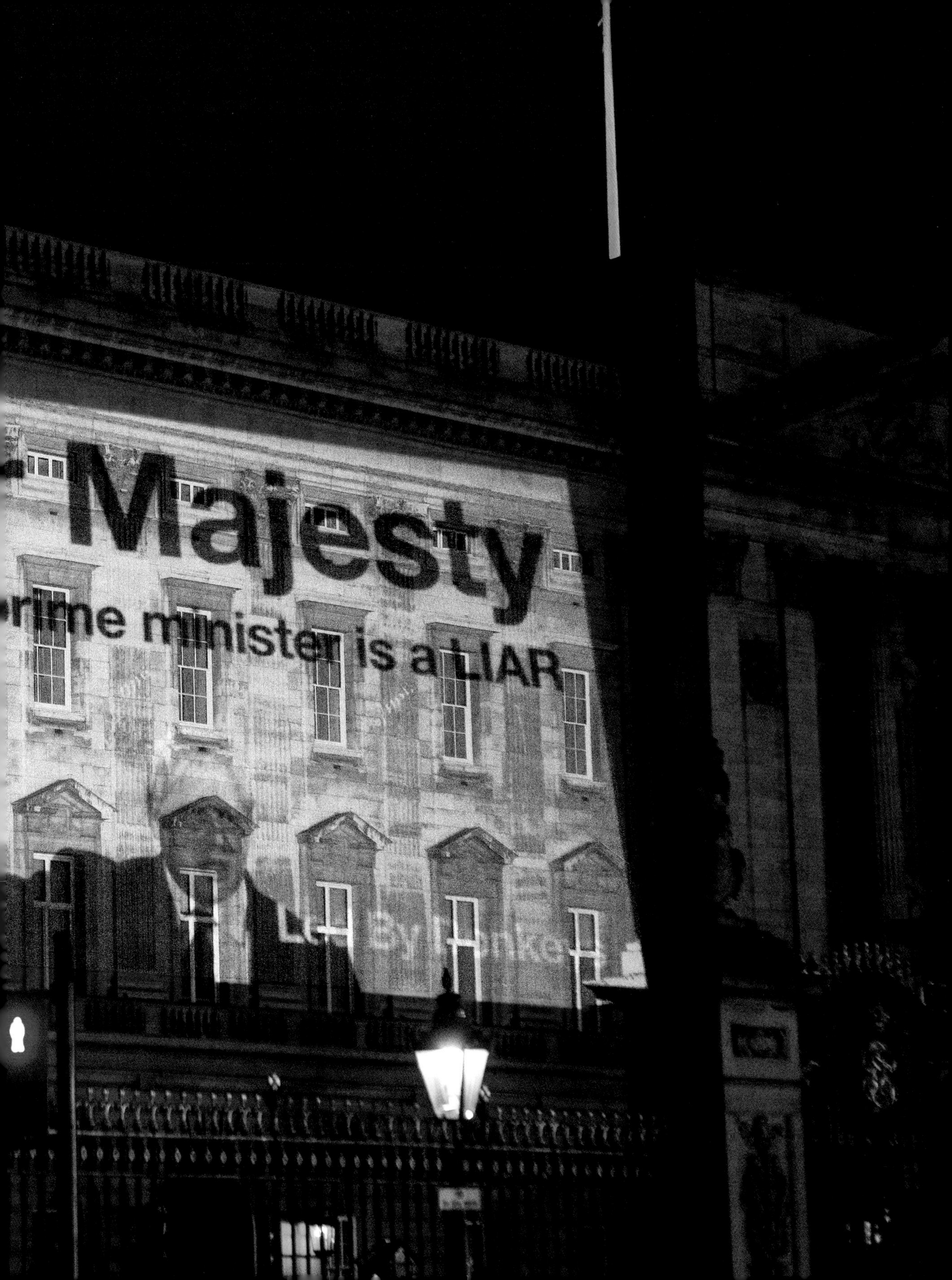
Majesty
rime minister is a LIAR

Boris Johnson

One of the worries was that an armed police officer might mistake our projector for something more sinister and overreact as we aimed it squarely at Buckingham Palace.

Boris Johnson was due there in a few hours to be appointed by the Queen to the office for which he'd strived for most of his life. Knowing that the building was heavily protected, we'd devised a plan to project a single still image onto the building from the back of a vehicle, snap a quick photo, then speed away. The picture would be of Johnson holding a kipper in the air, above the words: 'YOUR MAJESTY, YOUR NEW PRIME MINISTER IS A LIAR.'

The deployment of a fish, which made sense at the time, was related to mooted post-Brexit food regulations. More substantively, we wanted to do something to mark the moment this man became PM. The nation had for some time been subjected to a deluge of sycophantic drivel by his media outriders ('NOW BRING US SUNSHINE' drooled a *Daily Mail* front page when he won the Tory leadership), so it seemed important to us to proclaim that the Emperor was, in fact, naked. He was a rogue. A charlatan. The Emperor was a proven bullshit artist who belonged nowhere near the levers of power.

As it was, the level of security around the palace meant our plan had to change and we ended up parking on a side road, then navigating multiple residential streets with a huge projector and generator, occasionally stopping and feigning innocence as police patrol cars passed by. Eventually we reached the palace just as, somewhat portentously, an electrical storm crackled above our heads.

The generator hummed, the lens cap came off and a moment later the facade of Buckingham Palace was filled with a photo of Johnson triumphantly holding aloft the fish above our message to Her Majesty. Suddenly armed police were rushing towards our team. Hands were thrust into the air just as the sky was pierced by a jagged bolt of white lightning. It seemed the gods themselves were as offended as the rest of us by Johnson's imminent ascension.

And who could blame them? He was about to be appointed to a role of immense power. Boris Johnson, the faux-bumbling clown from *Have I Got News for You*, would later that day be asked to write a letter to the captains of Britain's Trident submarines, instructing them on whether or not to launch an atomic counterstrike if Britain was nuked. He would command a seat on the UN Security Council. He would be in charge of the world's fifth largest economy and yet he seemed to us to be a vainglorious semi-adolescent who lied with the ease and comfort of a romance scammer.

The police led our team away and issued various empty threats of prosecution and confiscation, but soon our photo was online and running across the media. Even now it is a point of pride that we publicly called him a liar across the front of Buckingham Palace on the morning he became prime minister.

We knew who he was, millions of us did, and in the first months of his premiership he did nothing to disabuse us. And so, there was a sense of foreboding knowing he was in charge when reports emerged of a new flu-like virus causing mass fatalities in China. Early in March 2020, as the wave was about to break over Britain, Johnson declared: 'I was at a hospital the other night where I think there were a few coronavirus patients and I shook hands with everybody, you'll be pleased to know.'

The Emperor, it seemed, was also an idiot.

It was at this point that we began documenting his Covid decision-making – a project that would find form in an extensive timeline of failure that was presented on our website Appeasement.org and accompanied by a billboard depicting Johnson as the antithesis of his hero, Winston Churchill.

Our timeline was wholly fact-based, no editorialising, just a deeply-sourced list of events, but when read in its entirety it revealed something new about the depths of incompetence to which Johnson had stooped as Covid raged. Five missed COBRA meetings at the outset of the crisis, the flirtation with herd immunity, stopping mass testing and contact tracing 11 days before the first lockdown … It was all there, in day-by-day detail. Then, when it was revealed that his chief lieutenant Dominic Cummings had driven north with his family while infected – completely at odds with Johnson's self-penned regulations – and when the prime minister then backed Cummings and gaslit a nation, we turned the timeline into a film narrated by ex-*Newsnight* anchor Gavin Esler before heading with the projector to Barnard Castle in County Durham.

The tall illumination lamps that lit up the northern wall of the castle – the site we chose to project our film – threatened to scupper the intervention, but a master key (procured for such occasions) fitted the lamps' control boxes and we turned them off before firing up the projection (see page 66). Many millions of online views later it had become clear there was a real appetite for this kind of guerrilla journalism – the presentation of hard facts in a compelling fashion. Much of what we were reporting was not new, but there was something about our country's collective diminishing attention span and denuded medium-term memory, combined with the pure volume of information to which we were all subjected during the pandemic, that meant it was hard to grasp a complete picture of Johnson's failures. But for whatever reason, our film did just that.

While researching the appeasement timeline, we'd come across one of those simple facts that makes you stop still and blink. Now, we're not prudish, and of all Johnson's personal and political calumnies, his sexual peccadilloes were of the least concern to us. But nevertheless, it was a tea spitter to learn that on at least five occasions he'd got a woman pregnant while being married to someone else. And as we dug deeper, we found more examples of his personal and political debasement. So, we began writing an exhaustive biopic of the man, from the moment he was born to the day he became prime minister.

Our new film listed lie after lie, interspersed with examples of Johnson's cruelty and corruption (see page 128). Again, much of what we were reporting was not new, but by piecing it together as a series of time-ordered facts, the impact was stark. The film would eventually be watched around 20 million times and this simple technique of chronologically listing the facts in five- or ten-minute social media films was soon aped by the BBC.

It came as no surprise when, at the end of 2021, it emerged that Johnson had been a serial breaker of his own lockdown rules. He'd ridden to power on the back of a newly-minted flavour of political snake oil that his media allies labelled 'boosterism'. Britain was exceptional, we could have it all, no trade-offs, no compromise with reality. You just needed to *believe* in Britain. But it turned out Britain still believed in the rules and it was Partygate that eventually did for Boris Johnson.

In a country riven by inequality, where hard-working people could barely make ends meet, where public services were breaking and trust in institutions was crumbling, it was unsurprising that Johnson's confected optimism, however cynical, had found an audience. But by the end of his tenure our country was coarsened, brazen lying had become a routine political tactic, loyal fools held the great offices of state, a pandemic had been bungled and corruption was rampant.

The political scientist Peter Hennessy has articulated the 'good chap theory' of government – that Britain, without a codified constitution, relies on our leaders to restrain themselves and act within informal boundaries set by convention. In other words, shame alone is enough to make our leaders govern with integrity. But what happens when the person who makes it to Number 10 is, in fact, shameless?

After Boris Johnson went to Buckingham Palace that morning, we all found out.

Deal or No Deal

REDCAR, NORTH YORKSHIRE / UK

The third guerrilla poster we put up, back in January in Romford, was a Gove quote from the Brexit campaign: 'The day after we vote to leave, we hold all the cards and we can choose the path we want.' Well, it turned out the cards were held not by us but by the world's biggest single market. By September 2019 the government, of which Gove was a leading member, was bemoaning supposed EU blackmail and saying Britain may now have to leave without a deal. Ministers claimed the referendum provided a mandate for a no-deal Brexit and there was even an official (and expensive) billboard campaign warning us it might be about to happen.

But hang on, hadn't Gove said the opposite of that six months earlier in a little-noticed newspaper article? We resolved that the quote should now be made famous, to expose the lie at the heart of the no-deal threat. We brought the quote to one of the communities that would be most impacted by a no-deal Brexit and rendered it so large that it could be seen from space.

Johnson vs The NHS

SAUNTON SANDS, NORTH DEVON / UK

Having promised an extra £350m a week investment into the NHS on the side of his red bus, Johnson was now promising to build 40 new hospitals in a decade. Subsequent events have demonstrated it was a pledge the Conservatives had no intention of honouring, but even at the time it was clear it was another exercise in Johnson sophistry.

We joined forces with nurses and junior doctors to rake out a message to Britain. The technique for mapping a message this large is a trade secret held by the friends who helped us pull this off. What we can say is that it involved satellites and cricket stumps.

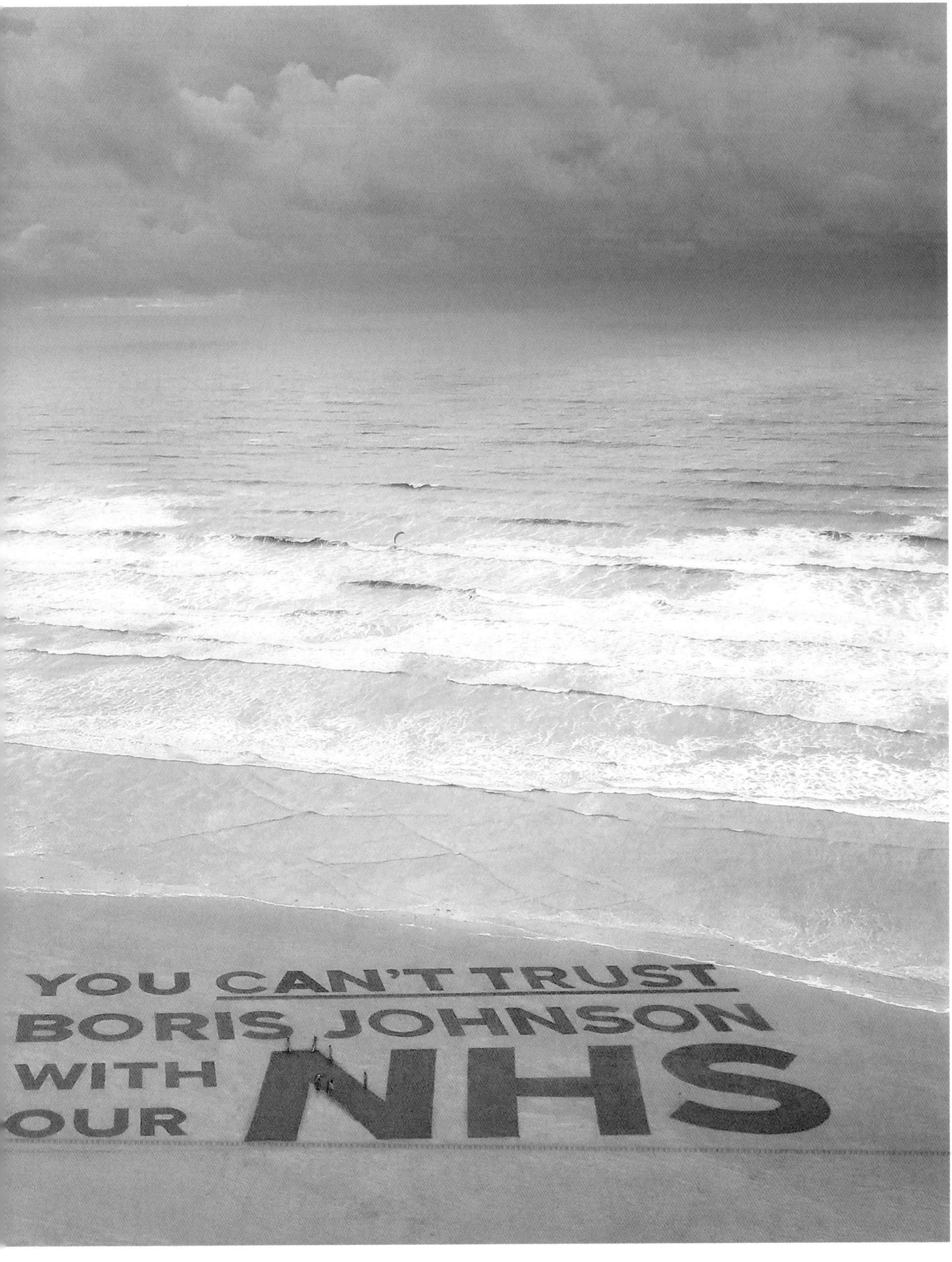
YOU CAN'T TRUST
BORIS JOHNSON
WITH
OUR
NHS

The Field

Months of Brexit political chaos had shifted the national mood and a clear majority of the country now wanted to remain in Europe. But how to land that fact and in a way that might appeal to the broadest possible audience?

Our idea was to plough an unmissable message into the British landscape. The intervention would also tell the story of 'leave' voter Lisa Dodd, who like countless others had changed her mind, explaining why she felt cheated by Nigel Farage and now wanted a second vote. Our film included an epic aerial reveal of our message deep in the English countryside set to Elgar's 'Nimrod'.

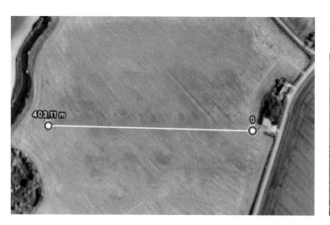

00:00:08:21

00:00:19:13

00:01:08:14

00:01:14:14

A YouGov analysis of 300 polls show
a majority of Britons would now vote
to stay in the European Union.

Lisa Dodd is one of them.

00:00:04:22
I voted leave because of the NHS. I just can't believe I fell for it.

00:00:12:24
Manipulated, wasn't I? Well and truly. Wonder how many more.

00:00:20:13
People say to me 17.4 million people voted for this and that's what they want. I'm one of those 17.4 million and that is not what I want. That is not what I voted for.

00:00:34:16
I want my vote back. I've had my vote stolen. I want it back.

00:01:23:00
I think it was Nigel Farage says the other day that there's no point in having another vote because it would be even more leave now than it was before. No, you know that it wouldn't. And that's why you don't want us to have it.

Projecting on Parliament

SOUTH BANK, LONDON / UK

The Houses of Parliament provide an excellent canvas for projections, both for the direct political resonance and because the building itself is stunning, perhaps even more so when floodlit at night. We've always felt that a well-crafted message on Parliament speaks not just to MPs and Lords, but to the country at large.

Over the years our projections on Parliament have become progressively harder to pull off as our cat and mouse relationship with the police has hotted up. The police will step in pretty quickly to shut down a projection and have on occasion confiscated equipment.

We've developed a range of tactics for getting our equipment onto the South Bank and into position unseen so we can deliver our projections quickly, before the police have time to organise a response. It doesn't always work out.

Wedlake Bell

TheBrexitParty.com

TAUNTON, SOMERSET / UK

When Farage's new party failed to publish a manifesto for the European elections, we wrote it for them based on the previous statements of their leading figures. We also registered the website thebrexitparty.com and posted the manifesto there.

Months later we received an eight-page legal letter from Farage's lawyers, Wedlake Bell, coming after us for copyright and intellectual property infringement. We were amused to note Farage was using European law to challenge our ownership of the site.

In a spirit of goodwill and Christmas cheer we offered to give it to him. For £1m. All proceeds to the Joint Council for the Welfare of Immigrants (the price went up by £50,000 a day).

Neither he nor his lawyers replied. We still own the site.

2020

Veterans on the Cliffs

DOVER, KENT / UK

31 January 2020, the final day of Britain's membership of the European Union. Farage and Co were planning a fiesta of nationalism in London, but many of his compatriots were deeply upset at the prospect of Britain's departure from a project that, they felt, represented an effort to secure the peace. Among them were Sidney 'Sid' Daw and Brigadier Stephen Goodall, both World War II veterans. They had a message for the people of Europe that we projected onto the White Cliffs of Dover. The film ended with a message to the continent: 'This is our star. Look after it for us.'

I feel really depressed at the idea that we are leaving Europe

SID: I'm Sid, I'm 95 years of age. I'm an ex-World War II veteran.

STEPHEN: My name is Brigadier Stephen Goodall. I am now nearly 98 years old.

SID: So what I would like to say to you now in Holland and in Germany and France, Belgium, everybody, this is a message from the White Cliffs of Dover. From Britain.

STEPHEN: I feel really depressed at the idea that we are leaving Europe because it has meant so much to me.

SID: I feel very very sad about it all because you don't know which way things are going.

STEPHEN: I like to be called a European and the feeling that one has of comradeship as one goes round Europe is really quite something.

SID: First of all I'm Welsh and I'm British and I'm European and I'm a human being.

STEPHEN: At my age I shan't be living much longer. But I hope that for the sake of my children and my grandchildren and my great-grandchildren that England, Britain, will move back to be much closer to Europe than what we have done now.

SID: So let's all think of these lovely cliffs. Look from your side to this side, see these white cliffs and we're looking across at you feeling we want to be together, and we will be together before long I'm sure.

Making Big Ben Bong

WESTMINSTER, LONDON / UK

The week before Brexit day had witnessed one of those spirit-sapping political spats in which Nigel Farage had castigated the authorities for failing to ensure Big Ben could chime at 11pm to signal the moment of Britain's departure from the EU (the Elizabeth Tower was being renovated). We were determined to make Farage's fervent wish come true and formulated a plan to bring Big Ben to life.

After procuring Euronews lanyards and dressing up the projector kit as high-end camera equipment (to avoid interest from a strong police presence), we moved into place on Westminster Bridge. As Farage celebrated a few hundreds metres away, at 11pm precisely the tower regained a (projected) clock face and the bongs rang out, before the clock morphed into a video of some of Farage's Brexit absurdities.

The Pandemic Begins

MULTIPLE LOCATIONS / UK

Brexit Day, 31 January, saw the first confirmed Covid case in the UK. Very early on in the pandemic it became clear that many people would continue to undertake essential public service, often at very real risk to themselves, while others saw the crisis as an opportunity to turn a profit. It was also apparent that Johnson's decision-making was in stark contrast to the approach of more experienced leaders.

Appeasement

KENTISH TOWN, LONDON / UK

As it became clear Johnson was botching the pandemic, we produced a detailed written timeline laying out his incompetence. To host the timeline we registered the url Appeasement.org – reflecting the disconnect between Johnson's image of himself (once-in-a-generation talent redolent of Churchill) and the reality (out of his depth). Johnson wasn't the only contemporary political figure that featured in our re-working of the famous image of Chamberlain returning from Munich.

Barnard Castle

COUNTY DURHAM / UK

After our Covid timeline exposing Johnson's failures had proved valuable to journalists and the wider public, we considered turning it into a film. The impetus for getting it done was Johnson's implacable support for his *consigliere* Dominic Cummings after it was revealed he'd driven north while infected with Covid, breaking the lockdown rules that Downing Street had imposed on the rest of us. Johnson had a choice – back his aide or back the public health messaging at the core of the nation's Covid response. He chose the former.

We made the film and – once regulations allowed it – followed in the footsteps of Cummings' notorious vision-testing journey to project it at the scene of the crime.

Stay Alert

WESTMINSTER BRIDGE ROAD, LONDON / UK

Few will forget the government's chevron-heavy appeals for us to stay alert to the virus. The smaller billboard is a graph of comparative nations' Covid death rates.

We Will All Suffer

KENTISH TOWN, LONDON / UK

The government's Covid billboard campaign was ripe for satire when Dominic Cummings' adventures at Barnard Castle were revealed.

MAR
27

Johnson and Cummings have coronavirus

Black Lives Matter

WESTMINSTER BRIDGE ROAD, LONDON / UK

At a time when it was difficult to protest publicly because of the pandemic, together with BLM UK organisers and leading anti-racism campaign groups, we put up a poster listing more than 3,000 names of people who had died in police custody, prisons, immigration detention centres and in racist attacks in the UK.

A Refugee's Story

DOVER, KENT / UK

Sitting atop the White Cliffs of Dover wearing sunglasses and with his shirt tucked into his shorts, Nigel Farage had taken to filming refugees coming ashore on Britain's Channel coast. He would then post his videos to his social media with incendiary commentary, inevitably fomenting hatred and division. Some newspapers and Home Secretary Priti Patel followed in his wake, sparking one of Britain's periodical panics about desperate people seeking safety here, at the core of which was a failure to recognise the humanity of the people being targeted.

We invited Syrian refugee Hassan Akkad, who had crossed a sea on his way to Britain, to tell his story from the cliffs. The following day he was invited onto multiple TV shows, where viewers heard from one of the people Farage was seeking to demonise.

00:00:00:00 - 00:00:24:13

Hello, everyone. Apologies for taking over the cliff, but I have a few words that I would love to share with you. My name is Hassan and five years ago I was on the other side of this channel trying to cross here. These cliffs were actually visible from our makeshift camp and they represented hope. Hope that I would live a safe and stable life here in Britain having fled my war-torn country.

00:00:24:13 - 00:00:50:12

Similar to those that are arriving recently, I had to put my trust in a people smuggler because a safe and a legal option to seek asylum here was and still is unavailable. Crossing the sea in a rubber dinghy is terrifying and devastating. Devastating because it makes you feel so helpless and insignificant. And I wouldn't wish it on my worst enemy.

00:00:50:14 - 00:01:14:23

Despite the growing number of people making the crossing to seek asylum here, Britain is not facing a refugee crisis. There are around 30 million refugees around the world, and Britain is home to only 1 per cent of them. Britain is, however, facing other crises, but we are being used again as a distraction from the actual crises facing this country caused by the people who are running it.

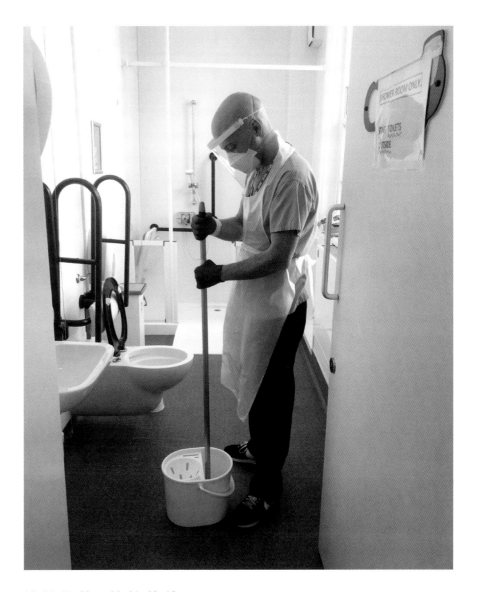

00:01:15:00 – 00:01:48:10

I will say it again. They are using us to distract you from how badly they have managed during this pandemic. The past few months have proved that the people who made Britain their home didn't hesitate to roll up their sleeves and keep this country running during the worst public health crisis in modern history. From harvesting our produce to stacking our shelves. From delivering our takeaways to looking after our elderly and sick. From driving our buses to, in my case, cleaning my hospital to help the NHS.

00:01:48:12 – 00:02:19:13

The only difference between you and us is luck. We did not choose for our countries to become so unsafe that even the deadly sea offered a better prospect. The past few months have proved that wherever we come from in the world, we are united by the love and concern we hold towards our loved ones. Just like you, we want what's best for us and for our families.

TRUMP
GOLF COUNT

08

JUL
3

U.S.
COVID DEATHS

132,3

Trump Golf Count

TRUMP TURNBERRY GOLF COURSE, SCOTLAND / UK

The elevation of Donald Trump to the US Presidency in 2017 handed the most powerful office in the world to a broken personality with authoritarian instincts. He was clearly a narcissist with a penchant for cruelty and a reverence for Putin, but when Covid struck, the greatest threat to the American people became his incompetence. As his compatriots died in huge numbers, Trump absconded himself from organising an effective response and instead concentrated on his swing. By the time we projected this film onto his course in Scotland in September 2020 he'd spent 24 days of the crisis playing golf. Two months later we gently nudged him to accept the result of November's election.

Covid-19 Bereaved Families for Justice

WESTMINSTER, LONDON / UK

Not long into the pandemic it became clear to many Britons that the crisis was being mishandled by the country's leaders. The sense that key decisions were being botched was felt most keenly by those whose loved ones had died. Jo Goodman and Matt Fowler didn't know each other before Covid struck but after both of them lost their dads, Stuart and Ian, they formed the group Covid-19 Bereaved Families for Justice to demand that lessons be learned. We allied with them to elevate their message, including this projection on Parliament featuring Lobby Akinnola, who lost his father Femi.

2021

The National Covid Memorial Wall

By spring 2021, nearly 140,000 Britons had lost their lives to Covid. It was such an extraordinary number, so vast it was barely possible to grasp. The virus had been raging for a year and the toll was unbearable.

A few months earlier a group of bereaved families had started desperately trying to share their experiences in the hope of convincing the government to run a 'rapid review' into the handling of the pandemic response so far. We approached the founders of Covid-19 Bereaved Families for Justice, Matt Fowler and Jo Goodman, to explore how we could help them elevate their important message. Together we made a short film, addressed to the prime minister, in which several members of their group spoke about their loss and what they thought had gone wrong. The film, projected onto the Houses of Parliament, was seen by hundreds of thousands of people and helped push the group further into the public spotlight (see page 80).

Keen to work together again, our conversation over the following weeks turned to how we might find a way to communicate the scale of the pandemic in the UK. The collaboration found new urgency and focus when it emerged that Boris Johnson was exploring creating a government-sanctioned national Covid memorial. Given Johnson's dire handling of the pandemic we all felt strongly that any public memorialisation should be in the hands of those who had lost loved ones, not those responsible for too many of those deaths.

Early in February 2021, the beginnings of an idea emerged. We wanted to create a living memorial, installed by people who had lost loved ones to the virus. And we wanted to build it in a place that would be accessible to grieving families and friends *and* be impossible for our political leaders to ignore.

We talked through many different ideas for how we might depict the scale of human loss. An early idea focused on laying down 140,000 pebbles or candles. But as the conversation progressed, we realised we wanted to create something less transient and the idea of a fixed, painted symbol emerged. Different concepts were considered – candle flames, hands, stars and others – before finally we landed on hearts, a powerful symbol of life and love.

But where should all of these hearts go? We knew we needed to marry two important components – a site for memorialisation that felt suitably dignified, but also a highly visible site that contained the political element that we all felt was an essential part of the installation. We trod the cold streets of central London looking for a good location. When we first descended the steps from Westminster Bridge onto the Albert Embankment we knew immediately that we had found it.

Lined with beautiful mature plane trees, this stretch of riverside walk between Westminster Bridge and Lambeth Bridge is relatively serene and peaceful for central London. Backed by a seven-foot-high wall that stretches for half a kilometre and faces directly out across the Thames to the riverside terraces of the Houses of Parliament, it couldn't have been more appropriate.

Our attention turned to calculations. We set about carefully measuring the length and height of the wall. It consisted of 26 separate panels, each more than 20 metres long and punctuated by pillars. With the number of Covid deaths in the UK approaching 140,000, that meant we needed to accommodate over 5,300 hearts in each panel over a length of nearly 500 metres.

With these intimidating figures still fresh in our minds we discussed using stencils to enable us to get large numbers painted quickly. We prepared some computer mock-ups, but standardised hearts made the wall look like it had been pasted in Hallmark wrapping paper. The stencil idea was dropped. It just didn't feel right. If this was to be a fitting memorial, each heart needed to be hand-painted, a unique mark of love and respect shown to the individual whose life it would represent.

At home in our gardens, experiments got underway with a huge variety of paints, brushes, art pens and applicators as we tested drawing hearts on different surfaces, including concrete slabs, stone surfaces and bricks. How quickly was it possible to paint a heart? How did the colours work on different surfaces? How long would it take for the paints to fade away in the rain and sun? There was a huge variation depending on the paint and the surface. But soon a front-runner emerged.

The humble Posca paint pen, much beloved of street and graphic artists the world over, was quick to use and its bright red colour held up well on stone. A decision made, we now needed to procure the thousands of Poscas we required, based on calculations for how many hearts each pen would paint before running out. We hit the phones – contacting street art festival organisers, stationary shops and wholesalers, in the UK and overseas. As we set about buying just about every Posca in the country, we noticed the price was creeping up each day. This, we thought, was an unfortunate coincidence, until we realised the source of the inflation was us. We'd cornered the market in red Posca pens and, together with a UK-wide shortage created by Brexit, were rapidly pushing up the cost of each pen. But soon, boxes of Poscas were flooding in.

Now we needed an effective plan for getting the hearts up on a wall when we didn't have permission to paint on it. To counter the risks involved, we developed a plan that would make the project look like an official and well-organised memorial site within minutes of our arrival at the wall. Our calculation was that if we dressed the site (and ourselves) appropriately, we'd make it very hard for the first police officer on site to intervene and force us to stop. And after painting hearts for just an hour or two, we thought, the project would become unstoppable. We needed to buy time, that was the calculation. But we had no idea if it would actually work.

All of this planning had been underway during the winter lockdown. We knew we could only install the memorial once Britain had opened up, so when the day for the lifting of the lockdown was announced, we had our date. 29 March 2021. Working closely with Covid-19 Bereaved Families for Justice we set about organising a group of 40 or so volunteers to participate in the all-important first day, where we would seek to take the site and get the installation underway.

On launch day we met at the Lambeth Bridge end of the wall opposite Lambeth Palace at 8.30am. Not so early that the embankment would be empty, not so late that we lost important hours of the first day. Our van arrived to drop off the essential kit and the first boxes of Posca pens. Everyone was nervous and keen to get started. Just before 9am we were ready to go.

Loaded with kit and wearing our bespoke 'Covid Memorial Wall' tabards and facemasks, we set off down the half-kilometre length of wall towards the start position. We all felt very conspicuous, the walk felt like it went on forever, but soon we were in place close to Westminster Bridge and our teams swung into action to make the site look official. Within minutes, our huge signs bearing the words 'The National Covid Memorial Wall' (painted in Farrow & Ball grey with gold lettering) had been fixed to the wall. Below them, large formal wreaths of flowers were laid on the ground. Alongside these we placed two large candle lanterns. Very quickly our A-frame sandwich boards, made to look like the sort of thing you might find outside a National Trust tea room and painted to match the wall signs, were set out in intervals along the first 150 metres of the wall. Volunteers with matching postcard flyers started to hand them out to passers-by. Other volunteers set about sweeping out the dirty gutter below the wall and bagging up the wet leaves and dirt. Meanwhile, Covid-19 Bereaved Families for Justice co-founder, Matt Fowler, was painting the very first heart in memory of his father, Ian. Soon afterwards red hearts were blossoming across the first three panels of the wall. We were underway.

But an hour or two in, it became clear we were going to need many, many more people painting hearts if the installation wasn't going to take weeks to complete. We exchanged glances, our nerves still palpable. We had started, but how on earth were we going to finish? Had we bitten off more than we could chew?

At least our livery had worked, as the police showed little interest in us. Covid-19 Bereaved Families for Justice put out a press release, sparking a flurry of online articles before TV and radio crews showed up at the wall to talk to family members. Moving photos of the wall started to travel on social media. Hearts were going up at a good pace. Hour by hour we felt the wall becoming increasingly unstoppable.

At around midday a representative from Lambeth Council turned up. Far from wanting to shut us down, he wanted to start a conversation about how the council could help. It felt promising. As the media coverage spread, new families and friends were arriving to put up their own hearts. Nurses and doctors from St Thomas' Hospital – many of whom had been on the frontline in Covid wards – started to come out to paint their hearts for lost family members or colleagues. At around 3pm, Leader of the Labour Party, Keir Starmer, arrived with his team and a large media scrum gathered around him. Now we had momentum.

Our small crew of volunteers pressed on through the afternoon into the early evening. Already there were thousands of beautiful hearts on the wall.

At the end of the day, we briefed the security patrol we had hired to keep an eye on the site through the night and headed back to a flat we had rented at the top of Lambeth Bridge Road as Project HQ. Exhausted but still buzzing with adrenalin, we found space to perch among boxes of thousands of Posca pens and reviewed day one over pizza and beers. We were elated at how well the day had gone, but we knew we had a problem to fix – how to bring in more people? At our current rate, the project was going to take until May to finish.

Early on day two we turned our attention to finding more volunteers. We had some recruits already in place, but based on progress from day one it was already clear that we needed more. Hundreds more. So we set up an Eventbrite – an online tool that allows people to book into timed events – and set about getting it seen far and wide.

Also emerging as a new challenge was how to keep track of our progress towards the target of 140,000 hearts. How would we know we had the right number of hearts painted to match data from the Office for National Statistics? We tried taking high-resolution photographs and manually counting, but it took forever and by the time we'd counted a panel, volunteers had arrived adding new hearts, rendering the count redundant. Then we heard about someone at The Massachusetts Institute of Technology who had developed software capable of counting distinct items in a pattern and we got in touch. This was the breakthrough we needed, meaning we could tally up each panel into a grand total at the end of each day with ease.

But something else happened on the second day. We had been so focused on delivering the plan and making sure we could hold the site for long enough that we weren't quite prepared for the transformation of the wall from a logistical operation to a place of memorialisation and with it, great emotion. From late on the first day and as the second day got underway, there was simply a huge amount of grief present at the wall. People who had held small and socially-distanced funerals for lost loved ones, if they had held them at all, were now coming to the wall to paint their heart. Families were sharing their grief publicly for the first time. Repeatedly, we heard people saying they had needed somewhere to go to express their loss, somewhere public, and that the wall was that place. Families or groups of friends were arriving with cava to toast loved ones, people were laying flowers along the length of the wall. No one who worked on the wall during those days was left unaffected by that huge outpouring of emotion.

By day three, news of the wall and our need for more volunteers to help paint hearts was travelling widely, with many new volunteers signing up.

Freshly painted hearts were going up all the time and individual sections between pillars started to fill up, allowing us to declare them 'closed' and pressing on to new sections. Slowly but surely, we were working our way up to the Lambeth Bridge end. And as the wall filled up with hearts, so it started to become visible from the other side of the Thames – a red wall of love visible from the riverside terraces of the Houses of Parliament.

At the end of each day before the light failed, we began the process of taking our high-resolution photos that would allow the digital counting overnight. On day nine it became clear we needed just one more day to reach our initial target of 140,000 unique hand-painted hearts.

Over a total of ten long days, battling every kind of springtime London weather, from blazing sun to horizontal snow, more than 1,200 people signed up to help install hearts across half a kilometre of wall. It was a monumental effort, but we'd achieved what we'd set out to do with the Covid-19 families – create a powerful and beautiful memorial built by the bereaved for the bereaved.

Throughout the installation and in the weeks and months that followed it, the wall began to land culturally and politically. Many MPs came to visit, some with their constituents. The Archbishop of Canterbury walked the wall with other faith leaders. Boris Johnson, who had refused to come down to meet representatives of Covid-19 Bereaved Families for Justice while it was being painted, eventually snuck down three weeks after its completion under cover of darkness and without an entourage. The following day Johnson announced a public inquiry into his government's handling of the pandemic, across the river at the dispatch box in the House of Commons.

Since its initial completion, the wall has remained highly visible in the media. Photographs of the memorial are still routinely used to illustrate stories about Covid. Perhaps most poignantly, in 2023 a photograph of the memorial was mounted on the wall of the Covid-19 Inquiry and could be seen above Dominic Cummings and Boris Johnson as they gave their evidence.

What happens next to the wall is still uncertain, but there is a well-organised campaign to preserve and protect it. Many MPs from different parties have called for it to be made permanent. What is certain is that the wall continues to be loved and cherished as a living memorial. Every week a group called The Friends of the Wall (that includes many of the people who helped install it) meet to repaint fading hearts and add the new hearts needed to represent those who continue to lose their lives to Covid.

Our involvement as Led By Donkeys remained unknown throughout the installation because we didn't feel it was relevant to the story. In fact, our connection was only made public around four months later. What we have always felt, and continue to feel, is that we could not have delivered this project alone and nor could Covid-19 Bereaved Families for Justice. It was only possible as a result of a close and trusting collaboration between our two groups.

If you haven't been to the wall, we encourage you to visit it. In walking its full length – and taking the time to stop and read some of the inscriptions made in the individual hearts – its full power is realised. It is a story of loss, of grief and of love. And it offers a cautionary tale about the dangers of elevating to power politicians characterised by arrogance, complacency and incompetence.

The Wall

The site of the wall was a very deliberate choice. Together with
our collaborators, Covid-19 Bereaved Families for Justice, we chose
the Embankment opposite Parliament. The wall would primarily be
a memorial, but we also wanted its installation to be a political act,
a reminder to those in power that the choices being made in
Westminster were having a far-reaching and sometimes
devastating effect on families across the country.

Installing the wall was the culmination of weeks of planning.
We worked out the surface area we'd need to cover then
experimented with different paint and pens before putting in
an order that cornered the market in red Poscas.

By the time the final day of drawing was upon us, more than one
thousand volunteers had answered our call-out and the wall
stretched half a kilometre down the Embankment.

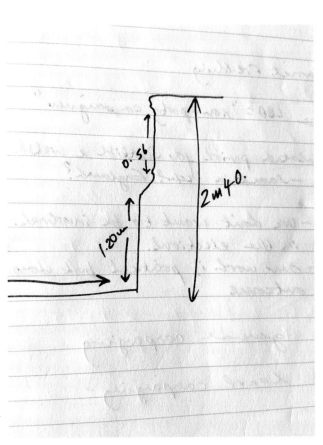

The Wall

The Observer
18 | 07 | 21

the new review

On the eve of 'freedom day', Dorian Lynskey tells the remarkable story of how grieving families created a memorial to those lost to Covid

WALL OF LOVE

150,000 AND COUNTING...

THE NATIONAL COVID MEMORIAL WALL

AFTER BANKSY

The wall became a focal point for national grief and was visited by opposition leader Keir Starmer, his deputy Angela Rayner and London Mayor Sadiq Khan.

When Archbishop of Canterbury Justin Welby visited the wall, he urged the public to walk its length and contemplate the scale of loss it signified. It was something Boris Johnson did only belatedly and after pressure, coming down in the dead of night in a move seen by the families as an effort to avoid them and their questions.

Nevertheless, Johnson could not avoid the wall when he gave evidence at the UK Covid-19 Inquiry two years later.

We took a series of high-resolution shots that were stitched together to form one unbroken image of the wall, allowing people to walk the wall virtually at walk.nationalcovidmemorialwall.org

Look Her in the Eyes

GLOUCESTER, GLOUCESTERSHIRE / UK

Health Secretary Matt Hancock broke his own social distancing rules to conduct an affair with PR operative Gina Coladangelo. Of more interest to us, Hancock made her a non-executive director at the Department of Health & Social Care, with no public record of the part-time appointment, which came with a taxpayer-funded fee of £15,000 for 15 days work. Our billboard was a spoof of Hancock's own Covid information posters.

GB News

SOUTHAMPTON, HAMPSHIRE / UK

Farage was using his show on GB News to attack RNLI lifeboat crews for providing a 'taxi service' to refugees crossing the Channel. Our campaign put a spotlight on the companies advertising on the channel and thus paying Farage's wages.

Brexit Reality Bites

MULTIPLE LOCATIONS / UK

As the failure of Brexit became increasingly evident, we got out with the ladder and brush again.

LOOK HER IN THE EYES

AND GIVE HER A
TAXPAYER-FUNDED JOB

RESIST › GOVERNMENT › CORRUPTION

Stop Aquind

Local residents in Portsmouth were campaigning against a new
undersea power cable that was described as unnecessary and a
threat to national security. Why then was the project going ahead?
It turned out that the owner of the company behind the plan,
Alexander Temerko, was a good friend and sometime drinking
partner of then prime minister Boris Johnson. Temerko and his
businesses had donated to one in ten Conservative MPs.
Our projection in Portsmouth named the MPs and the sums
they had received, in total £1.5m.

Jesus, Mary and Joseph led by the wee donkey

who exactly does the Metropolitan Police work for, ma'am?

my team are bringing that evidence direct to Scotland Yard.

LBD-12

Line of Duty

NEW SCOTLAND YARD, LONDON / UK

While teenagers and students had been fined thousands of pounds for attending illicit gatherings (some were still paying off penalties years later), the PM was not even the subject of an investigation by the Metropolitan Police.

Surely this was a case for AC-12. *Line of Duty*, the drama about a crusading police anti-corruption unit, was the most popular show on TV. We'd seen a tweet from the programme's creator and writer, Jed Mercurio, in which he'd slated Johnson, so we dropped Jed a line telling him we intended to park a huge TV screen outside Scotland Yard and blast a *Line of Duty*-themed film at the building. Jed quickly replied, offering to collaborate on our script and recruit Adrian Dunbar (Superintendent Ted Hastings) to voice it.

It was shared nearly 100k times on Twitter alone and made the newspaper front pages.

2022

AC-12 Returns

INTERVIEW ROOM, LINE OF DUTY / UK

After AC-12's visit to Scotland Yard had a huge impact we were soon collaborating with *Line of Duty* creator Jed Mercurio on a second film, this time putting Johnson in the interview room to be quizzed by Hastings, DI Steve Arnott and DC Kate Fleming. It felt cathartic to see Johnson finally grilled by the police and it seemed Britain felt the same way. The film circulated on thousands of street WhatsApp groups and was shown on ITV's *This Morning*. A week later the Met opened an investigation into 12 Downing Street parties.

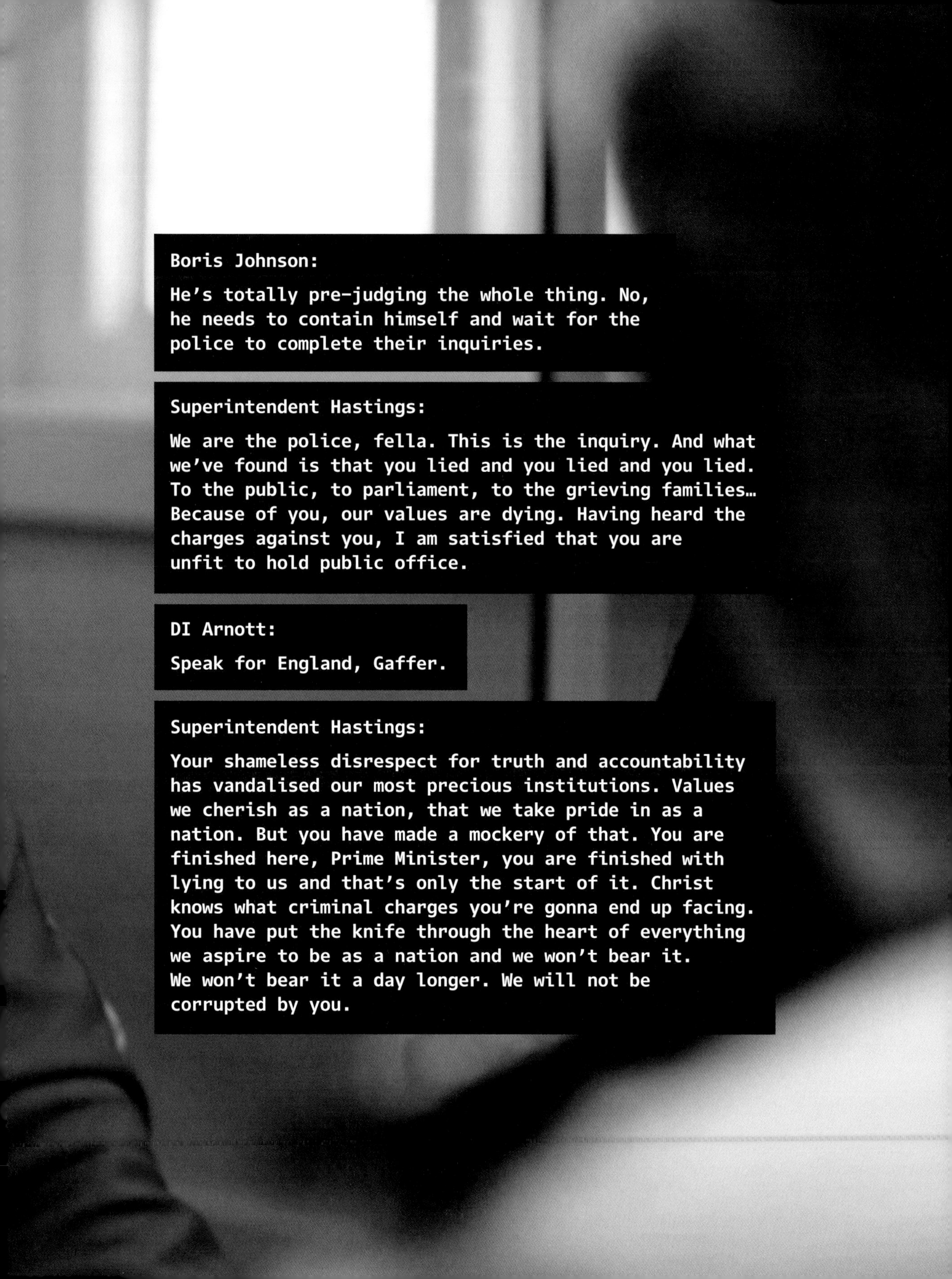

Boris Johnson:

He's totally pre-judging the whole thing. No, he needs to contain himself and wait for the police to complete their inquiries.

Superintendent Hastings:

We are the police, fella. This is the inquiry. And what we've found is that you lied and you lied and you lied. To the public, to parliament, to the grieving families… Because of you, our values are dying. Having heard the charges against you, I am satisfied that you are unfit to hold public office.

DI Arnott:

Speak for England, Gaffer.

Superintendent Hastings:

Your shameless disrespect for truth and accountability has vandalised our most precious institutions. Values we cherish as a nation, that we take pride in as a nation. But you have made a mockery of that. You are finished here, Prime Minister, you are finished with lying to us and that's only the start of it. Christ knows what criminal charges you're gonna end up facing. You have put the knife through the heart of everything we aspire to be as a nation and we won't bear it. We won't bear it a day longer. We will not be corrupted by you.

Sacrifice vs Sauvignon

MULTIPLE LOCATIONS / UK

By early 2022 it was clear just how great the extent of partying
at Downing Street during the lockdowns had been.

Invasion of Ukraine

BAYSWATER, LONDON / UK

On 24 February Putin ordered 150,000 troops to cross the border and invade Ukraine. It was an imperialist adventure designed to subjugate 38 million people. That day we projected a message onto the Russian Embassy in London from Daria Kaleniuk, an anti-corruption campaigner based in Kyiv. Her message was to the UK government: 'Russian oligarchs, they own London, they buy the most expensive villas and mansions in Great Britain, in London. These oligarchs empower Vladimir Putin, they make him an absolutely untouchable dictator. Putin is attacking now my country. So I beg you and I demand to stand up for Ukraine and impose targeted, tough sanctions right now. I demand block Putin's wallet now.' The police had some questions.

Partygate Crime File

It's hard to comprehend that the address at which more Covid lockdown breaches occurred than any other was the very same address where those laws were written. Our crime file, narrated by ex-*Newsnight* presenter and author Gavin Esler, detailed those breaches in exhaustive detail, including one drunken gathering that spilled into the Number 10 garden where revellers broke the prime minister's son's swing.

Our projection attracted the attention of the police (something that couldn't be said for Johnson's parties before pressure on Scotland Yard had forced a U-turn).

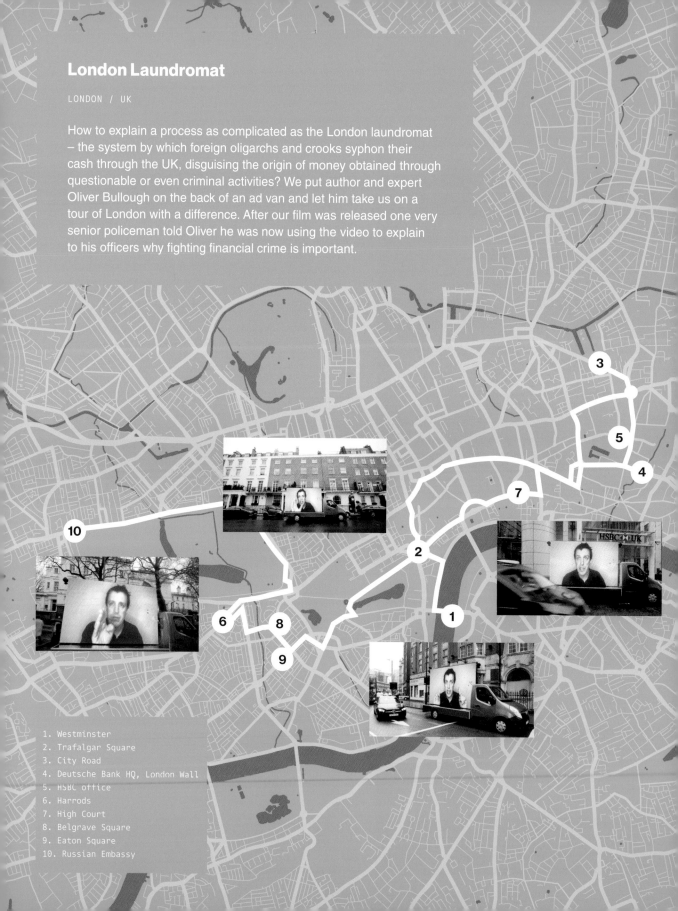

London Laundromat

LONDON / UK

How to explain a process as complicated as the London laundromat – the system by which foreign oligarchs and crooks syphon their cash through the UK, disguising the origin of money obtained through questionable or even criminal activities? We put author and expert Oliver Bullough on the back of an ad van and let him take us on a tour of London with a difference. After our film was released one very senior policeman told Oliver he was now using the video to explain to his officers why fighting financial crime is important.

1. Westminster
2. Trafalgar Square
3. City Road
4. Deutsche Bank HQ, London Wall
5. HSBC office
6. Harrods
7. High Court
8. Belgrave Square
9. Eaton Square
10. Russian Embassy

1. (00.05 - 00.18)

Hello. I'm going to show you how Putin's allies have spent billions of pounds of stolen money in London without getting caught — and how for years successive British governments have failed to take any meaningful action.

2. (00.42 - 01.15)

Okay, how does it work? Let's say you're a longtime Putin associate. Maybe you helped run St Petersburg together back in the 90s. And good news, he didn't forget you. In fact, Putin gave you control of a company he illegally seized from a political opponent. He needs his share to cement his position in power. But what about you? You've now got a billion dollars burning a hole in your pocket.

You need to access the most efficient scaled-up money laundering system in the world. You need London.

3. (01.15 - 01.48)

First things first, you need a UK-registered shell company. If you own your newfound wealth via a shell company, rather than in your own name, no one's going to know it's yours. 810,316 companies were created in the UK in 2023 – each one popping into life complete with limited liability, legal protections, property rights and all the rest of it. So where are all these companies? Well, 62,259 of them are in this one building on the City Road.

4. (03.45 - 04.06)

Fortunately Putin paid you your billion share in Cyprus, which is where all the Russian trades tend to get made. Now we need someone to move it from there to here. But who's going to do that? Relax, it's fine, this is London.

In 2017, Deutsche Bank was penalised $600m over a $10bn Russian money-laundering scheme that involved its New York, Moscow and London branches.

5. (04.07 - 04.18)

And this is HSBC. In 2012, HSBC Holdings was hit with a $1.9bn fine for activities, including serving as a conduit for Mexican drug cartels.

6. (04.41 - 05.05)

Okay, back to our billion dollars. We've stolen it, we've hidden it, we've moved it. Now we need to spend it. This is Harrods. And this is Zamira Hajiyeva. She's the wife of the former Chairman of the International Bank of Azerbaijan, and between 2006 and 2016 she used 54 different credit cards to spend £16.3m at Harrods.

7. (06.01 - 06.29)

But what if questions are asked about your stolen billion dollars? You're going to need to put a stop to that. But more good news – because Britain has the most stringent libel laws in the world, or some of them anyway. So you might want to try to throw some of your cash at one of the London law firms. Then you can drag any inconvenient authors and journalists here, to the High Court, where billionaires silence the people asking awkward questions.

8. (06.53 - 07.10)

Welcome to Belgravia. This is one of the most expensive postcodes on Planet Earth. And the good news is that for decades Britain hasn't just let shell companies buy houses here, it has let other countries' shell companies own property without ever having to say who the people behind them are.

9. (07.44 - 08.08)

Look at this place. It would have cost upwards of £10m. Who owns it? No idea, because it was bought by a company registered in the British Virgin Islands. Three doors down that way is registered in Panama. Three doors that way is in the Isle of Man. Opposite this place, the British Virgin Islands again. And next door to that? Guernsey.

10. (08.41 - 08.54)

The road from Moscow to Kyiv passes through Belgravia. For decades the London laundromat has helped keep Putin in power. It is one of the most spectacular British policy failures of the post-World War II era.

Disband the Met

NEW SCOTLAND YARD, LONDON / UK

The Metropolitan Police is a racist, misogynistic, homophobic, corrupt and incompetent organisation. Our 10-minute film, projected onto New Scotland Yard and narrated by Patsy Stevenson, who was violently arrested at the vigil for Sarah Everard, covered some of the most egregious examples of the Met's failings and its inability to reform itself. The film called for the institution to be disbanded and a new police force to be built in its place.

The Life and Lies of Boris Johnson

Our biopic of Boris Johnson's life, from the day he was born to the day he became prime minister, has been viewed 20 million times.

1964

Alexander Boris de Pfeffel Johnson is born in New York. His earliest recorded ambition is to become 'world king'.

1982

In a letter to Johnson's father, an Eton schoolteacher writes of the 17-year-old Boris Johnson: 'I think he honestly believes that it is churlish of us not to regard him as an exception, one who should be free of the network of obligation which binds everyone else.'

1983

Johnson becomes a leading member of Oxford University's male-only Bullingdon Club. During his tenure, the club's members indulge in sexist taunting, vandalism, restaurant trashing, bullying and ritual humiliation of the poor. One recruiter for the club will later describe it during Johnson's time, saying Bullingdon members 'found it amusing if people were intimidated or frightened by their behaviour. I remember them walking down a street in Oxford in their tails, chanting "Buller, Buller" and smashing bottles along the way, just to cow people ... Boris was one of the big beasts of the club. He was up for anything. They treated certain types of people with absolute disdain, and referred to them as "plebs".'

1984

Sixth-former Damian Furniss visits Johnson's Oxford college for his entrance interview. Many years later he will relate what happened: 'I was staying the night and had an evening to kill in the college bar. Johnson was propping up the bar with his coterie of acolytes whose only apparent role in life was to laugh at his jokes ... In the course of the pint I felt obliged to finish he mocked my speech impediment, my accent, my school, my dress sense, my haircut, my background, my father's work as a farm worker and garage proprietor, and my prospects in the scholarship interview I was there for. His only motivation was to amuse his posh boy mates.'

1987

At the age of 23, Johnson marries the daughter of a millionaire art historian. Fresh out of university and aided by family connections, he lands a traineeship at *The Times* newspaper.

1988

Johnson is sacked as a trainee by *The Times* for making up a quote on his first front-page story.

1991

According to a friend of Johnson's wife, an incident occurs in which Johnson displays his 'frightening temper', after which his wife turns up at the friend's flat in Brussels 'looking shocked, scared and on the brink of tears'. The marriage soon deteriorates as Johnson begins an affair with a barrister.

1993

Johnson gets his barrister girlfriend pregnant and is soon divorced for the first time.

1994

He is now a columnist for *The Telegraph* and *The Spectator* magazine. His columns include racially-charged invective, such as slamming Nelson Mandela for the 'tyranny of black majority rule' in post-apartheid South Africa and describing Chinese workers as, 'puffing coolies'.

1995

He describes the children of single mothers as, quote, 'ill-raised, ignorant, aggressive and illegitimate', saying it is, 'outrageous that married couples should pay for "the single mothers" desire to procreate independently of men'.

1999

Johnson is made editor of *The Spectator* magazine, promising owner Conrad Black that he will not stand to be an MP.

2000

Johnson begins a relationship with one of his employees. He promises her that he will leave his wife to marry her. He does not leave his wife.

2001

Breaking his promise to the owner of *The Spectator*, Johnson stands to be an MP. He now promises voters in Henley that if they vote for him he will step down as editor of *The Spectator*.

That June he becomes MP for Henley. He does not step down as editor of *The Spectator*.

In a book he writes during the election campaign, Johnson compares equal marriage to a union between 'three men and a dog.'

2002

Writing in *The Spectator*, Johnson defends British colonialism in Africa, saying, 'The problem is not that we were once in charge but that we are not in charge anymore ... Left to their own devices the natives would rely on nothing but the instant carbohydrate gratification of the plantain.' Meanwhile, in *The Telegraph*, he describes black Africans as 'flag-waving piccaninnies' with 'watermelon smiles'.

2004

Johnson is made vice-chair of the Conservative Party and shadow arts minister.

Rumours circulate that Johnson has got one of his employees pregnant, resulting in her having an abortion. Johnson slams the suggestion as, 'complete balderdash' and 'an inverted pyramid of piffle' and assures Conservative Party leader Michael Howard that the claim is untrue.

In reality, the rumours are entirely true. Johnson is sacked from his positions as Tory vice-chair and shadow minister for lying to the party leader.

2008

Johnson becomes Mayor of London.

2009

He fathers a child with an unpaid advisor to City Hall.

2013

The Court of Appeal throws out an injunction that has until now prevented Johnson being named as the father of the child. Three judges rule that the public has a right to know about Johnson's 'reckless' behaviour.

By now Johnson is having an affair with an American technology entrepreneur. Her company will receive £126,000 of public money while Johnson is Mayor.

2014

Johnson denies at least 17 times that he will stand as an MP while still in post as Mayor of London.

2015

Johnson stands as an MP while still in post as Mayor of London.

2016

Hedging his bets, Johnson drafts two Brexit articles: one pro-leave and the other pro-remain. In his pro-remain article, Johnson says the UK should remain, 'intimately engaged in the EU' and that Brexit could cause an 'economic shock', the diminishing of Britain on the world stage and the break-up of the Union.

Two days later Johnson announces he will be campaigning for Vote Leave.

On 23 June Britain votes to leave the EU. Prime Minister David Cameron resigns.

Johnson is the leading figure to replace him, but his leadership campaign soon implodes when his own campaign manager Michael Gove says that Johnson is, 'not capable' of 'leading the country'.

Instead Cameron is succeeded by Theresa May. She makes Johnson Foreign Secretary.

2018

Johnson resigns as Foreign Secretary and returns to his £250,000 a year job as a columnist for *The Daily Telegraph*.

Johnson is now having an affair with Carrie Symonds, a former Communications Director for the Conservative Party. Johnson and his wife will soon separate.

2019

Police are called to Symonds' south London flat after reports of a serious altercation. Neighbours report hearing a woman screaming, followed by slamming and banging. Symonds is reportedly heard screaming at Johnson to, 'get off me' and 'get out of my flat'.

Symonds will soon be expecting a baby. The relationship is Johnson's fifth extra-marital fling to be made public and the fifth time as a married man that he's made another woman, who isn't his wife, pregnant.

On 19 July, following an internal Conservative Party coup against Theresa May, Johnson fulfills his lifetime ambition and becomes Prime Minister of the United Kingdom.

Russian Oligarchs

KENSINGTON, LONDON / UK

We'd already produced a number of films about the Conservative Party's penchant for Russian money by the time Russia invaded Ukraine, so it didn't surprise us that the government was slow to impose sanctions on some of the London-based oligarchs who had been close to Putin.

A week after this intervention, Abramovich was finally subjected to UK sanctions.

Night at the Museum

SOUTH KENSINGTON, LONDON / UK

The Victoria and Albert Museum, one of the most famous cultural institutions in the world, is owned by all of us as a charitable public body. Trustees should be, and be seen to be, politically impartial and not occupy a high-profile role in a political party.

It was therefore something of a surprise to learn that at a Tory Party fundraising lunch, one prize was a private tour of the museum with then V&A Board Chair and Conservative Party supporter Nicholas Coleridge. Tory Party Chairman (and chief fundraiser) at the time, Ben Elliot, was also on the V&A board. Our gold-framed projection told the story and challenged the V&A to abide by its own code of conduct for Trustees.

00:00:00:00 - 00:00:08:29

Boris Johnson: The evidence is, Nick, that we would actually increase our exports to the EU if we came out of the legal legislative morass of the single market.

00:00:08:29 - 00:00:18:47

Jacob Rees-Mogg: There'll be no need for checks at Dover, but it will be an ability to ensure that the roads keep running around Dover even if there are delays at Calais. The delays will not be at Dover, they will be at Calais.

Delays and Denial in Dover

DOVER, KENT / UK

The powers of prediction demonstrated by our Brexit overlords had long been of interest to us before we took the ad van down to Dover. In July 2022 the roads approaching the port were jammed with lorry traffic – a situation that had been widely predicted, but dismissed by the leading Brexiteers. We made a film of their prophesies, put it on the giant screen and parked it in the queue. The following week Rees-Mogg was played his section of our film on the radio and was forced to admit: 'I got it wrong'.

00:00:18:47 – 00:00:32:07

Chris Grayling: We will maintain a free-flowing border at Dover. We will not impose checks in the port.

It was utterly unrealistic to do so. We don't check lorries now. We're not going to be checking lorries in Dover in the future. Absolutely clear. It can not happen.

00:00:32:07 – 00:00:47:32

David Davis: The sorts of fears being put up that there'll be problems on crossing from Dover to Calais.

The people in Calais, the port authorities, the leader of northern France, have all said that's not going to happen.

So there have been a lot of scare stories.

00:00:47:32 - 00:01:08:21

Dominic Raab: We want a bespoke arrangement on goods which recognises the peculiar, frankly, geographic economic entity that is the United Kingdom.

We are — and I hadn't quite understood the full extent of this — but if you look at the UK and you look at how we trade in goods, we're particularly reliant on the Dover-Calais crossing.

00:01:08:21 - 00:01:14:39

Boris Johnson: We say we can take back control. We can see the sunlit meadows beyond.

00:01:14:39 — 00:01:26:44

[Ends with Wagner's 'Ride of the Valkyries'.]

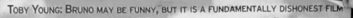
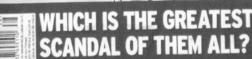

Hannan's Hypocrisy

BIRMINGHAM / UK

So-called 'godfather of Brexit' Daniel Hannan is one of the least insightful political commentators of modern times, having been more consistently wrong about issues of national importance than almost anyone. So naturally Boris Johnson elevated him to the House of Lords.

The Spectator vs Reality

DAGENHAM, LONDON / UK

The house magazine of Britain's political right exhibits a kind of detached superiority, like it somehow stands above the petty squabbles of the day. In reality, its prep school sensibility sees more value in needling the left than in being right. Its consistent denial of the science of climate change has played a significant part in radicalising the Conservative Party against action. We placed a giant banner of this front page from 2000 on a still-smouldering field in Dagenham, where an entire street had just gone up in flames in a record heatwave.

Tufton Street

Are you the chief executive officer of a tobacco company facing a hostile regulatory environment? Is the government planning to restrict your freedom to sell a deadly and highly addictive substance to teenagers? Naturally you're determined to prevent such a malicious measure being passed into law. But how? You could take to the airwaves, but nobody will treat you seriously – you run a tobacco company, you're the last person your press office would put on the radio.

Or perhaps you're the chairman of an oil company being targeted by protesters due to your decades-long misinformation campaign denying the link between fossil fuels and climate change. You want the government to strengthen the law around protest, restricting your opponents' ability to damage your brand, but you know you can't go on the television and propose such a move without inviting derision and further hostile coverage.

It's okay. Relax. You need a think-tank.

Specifically, you need one of the free-market think-tanks based in and around 55 Tufton Street in Westminster.

You already have a public affairs company on your books, managing your firm's reputation and engaging with politicians behind the scenes, but a free-market think-tank can do something different for you. It can take your case and present it to the public through the media and (this is the good bit) your involvement need never be revealed. Go to a donors' dinner, throw a think-tank some anonymous cash, then sit back and watch the BBC feature people whose wages you now pay advocating your company line. And all with fingerprints off.

Now, the people behind these 'think-tanks' (yes, let's put those words in inverted commas) would argue that they support your company's positions anyway, that you and they are ideological bedfellows, and that their advocacy has nothing to do with your recent financial contribution. And maybe that's true, but it's hard to tell because in general they don't reveal who their donors are so we can't be sure who they're representing on the airwaves. Only through dogged investigative journalism do we know that many of them are actually backed by oil and tobacco companies.

The Taxpayers' Alliance (TPA), the Global Warming Policy Foundation (GWPF), the Institute of Economic Affairs (IEA) and the rest of the Tufton Street crew act as corporate lobbyists while simultaneously holding a worldview shared by a tiny proportion of the public – extreme libertarian economics. At Led By Donkeys we all have backgrounds in climate campaigning and for years we've observed them promulgating scepticism or even outright denial around climate change while refusing to reveal the identities of the companies and individuals who pay for their campaigns.

But despite holding fringe beliefs on pollution, the NHS and tax (among other things), they long ago succeeded in co-opting a small cadre of journalists and activists to their cause. The problem is that those activists were, and still are, disproportionately members of the Conservative Party and its MPs. And few MPs were as zealous in their faith – and their familiarity with Tufton Street – as Liz Truss and Kwasi Kwarteng.

When 0.1 per cent of the British public (those Tory members) propelled Truss to power, she opened the door to an army of Tufton Street ideologues, staffing her Downing Street operation with 'think-tank' alumni who set about planning a mini-budget that would finally see their ideas implemented. When Kwarteng, Truss' Chancellor, delivered that mini-budget it was the apogee of three decades of corporate-funded campaigning designed to make an unpopular belief system into the governing ethos of Britain. He slashed corporation tax, abolished the top rate of income tax and introduced a host of other measures, long-demanded by 'think-tanks'. Tufton Street had won.

Soon after Kwarteng sat down in the Commons, one Conservative commentator tweeted: 'A massive moment for @IEAlondon. They've been advocating these policies for years. They incubated Truss and Kwarteng during their early years as MPs. Britain is now their laboratory.' Mark Littlewood, the director general of the Institute of Economic Affairs, replied with a self-important sunglasses emoji. Another journalist publicly asked: 'Has Liz Truss handed power over to the extreme neoliberal think-tanks?' To which the IEA's head of public policy replied, 'Yes'.

They say pride comes before a fall, and within hours the pound had crashed, mortgage rates were hiked and the cost of government borrowing dramatically increased – making most of us poorer and necessitating a series of humiliating U-turns.

But would they own it?

Nobody fails upwards quite like an extreme free-marketeer (see Brexit) but we were determined that blame for this one should land squarely on those responsible. We spent hours poring over Google Earth, trying to work out how to get onto the roof of 55 Tufton Street, from where we'd drop a huge banner declaring their culpability for this mess. Alas, the route we found over the roof tiles of Westminster appeared pretty perilous, and none of us was sure we wanted to sacrifice our lives for the cause of rinsing the Centre for Policy Studies. We decided instead to go up the front of the building on ladders and fix the giant banner by applying suction cups to the windows, but we were worried a gust of wind might catch the banner like a sail and pull out the glass. Finally, we decided to stick a blue plaque on the building – one of those small discs that you see on London townhouses denoting and honouring notable people in history who have lived in them. But to reflect the scale of the disaster visited on the country by these people, we'd make our plaque massive.

To tell the full story of the mini-budget we made a seven-minute film that we projected onto the building at midnight, then we returned at sunrise with our huge blue plaque. Two strangers had earlier spotted us manoeuvring it down a London street and called out, 'Hey, are you from Led By Donkeys?!' To which we'd stuttered an unconvincing denial, and by 7am we were on a backstreet in Westminster squeezing two tubes of extra-strong glue onto the back of our plaque before lifting the ladder into place and slapping the huge disc against the brickwork, then holding it in place until the glue dried.

With sirens wailing in the distance, we quickly lowered the ladder and dispersed. As the early morning rolled on, various 'think-tank' staffers arrived for work, looking up as they approached number 55 before stopping and taking a deep, heavy breath then slouching into the building. By mid-morning a top window was opened and various efforts were made to peel off the plaque. But the glue had done its job. The giant blue plaque was as resolute as the stain on Tufton Street's reputation.

For decades the 'think-tanks' had been producing pamphlets and reports laying out what they would do if they were in charge. Over countless appearances on the Today Programme and Question Time they had told us it was all very simple, we should just implement their agenda before marvelling at the resultant economic bounty. Now, almost immediately after assuming power, a prime minister had enacted their agenda with disastrous results.

It had taken Tufton Street just three weeks to crash the British economy.

The UK Economy Was Crashed Here

TUFTON STREET, LONDON / UK

Windows are the enemy of effective projections. Unless the curtains are pulled, even 50,000 lumens of light will pass through the glass and leave a gaping black hole in our canvas. So how to project a film onto the Georgian facade of 55 Tufton Street, exposing the building's inhabitants – the 'think-tanks' that conceived Liz Truss's disastrous mini-budget?

We constructed a giant mobile screen that we held up against the building, then projected the film. After a break while we waited for the sun to rise, we returned with a ladder, a blue plaque and two tubes of extra-strong glue.

Faragenomics

SALISBURY, WILTSHIRE / UK

Once the mini-budget had imploded the UK economy, we reminded the public who its biggest cheerleaders were.

Rish!

LEYLAND, LANCASHIRE / UK

By the time Sunak was running for the leadership of the Conservative Party in July, he was well-practised in using catchy campaign messages and slick images. As Chancellor, when he was in the relatively comfortable position of handing out large amounts of money during the pandemic, these images would often, memorably, carry his trademark signature. When 'Get Ready for Rishi!' signs started to appear as part of his leadership campaign, we saw the perfect opportunity to remind the country that, yet again, we would have a new Conservative prime minister in post who only a tiny number of people – this time not even Tory members, just MPs – had chosen.

Iranian Embassy

SOUTH KENSINGTON, LONDON / UK

Protests flared in Iran after the death of Mahsa Amini, killed by the country's morality police after being arrested for allegedly not wearing her hijab properly. Thousands of brave demonstrators, including many young women and girls, took to the streets under the slogan 'Woman. Life. Freedom.'

Our projection in London showed protesters who'd been killed in the regime's brutal crackdown. The footage was of them in happier times set to the protest song 'Baraye', which had become the soundtrack of the movement.

Covid VIP Lane

It remains something of a mystery that the Palace of Westminster was not, at least once in the last five years, surrounded by a teeming revolutionary mass of voters set upon the overthrow of the government. From the never-ending lies to the corruption of national institutions, to the flagrant lawbreaking inside Downing Street and the serial defenestration of prime ministers and the elevation in their place of various unelected oddballs … we seem as a nation to have endured so much without ever taking to the streets with a passion that would unnerve Number 10. But this failure to storm the barricades is perhaps most surprising when viewed through the lens of the Conservative Party's VIP lane for procuring personal protective equipment (PPE).

A brief summary: while doctors and nurses struggled, and in many cases died, serving on the Covid frontline, they often had to wear bin bags because of a national shortage of PPE. Meanwhile, the government ignored offers from many experienced PPE suppliers in favour of awarding contracts to the party's friends and donors. A VIP lane was set up that fast-tracked the Tories' associates, allowing them to land deals of staggering value, despite them often having no experience of actually procuring PPE. The unit price paid for items under VIP lane contracts was up to four times higher than the average, while government auditors found that suppliers with links to politicians were ten times more likely to be awarded contracts than those without political links.

There was Matt Hancock's local pub landlord, who secured a £40m contract to produce vials for Covid test kits, despite having no previous experience of supplying medical equipment (eight million of his tubes failed Health Department safety tests and were later burned). An adviser to Liz Truss secured a £252m contract for a company he worked for (facemasks supplied by the company worth £156m were deemed unsafe

and never used). A former aide to Priti Patel secured facemask contracts worth £103m, despite concerns in Whitehall that the taxpayer was paying over the odds. A former Conservative councillor who landed a £276m contract declared himself 'chuffed' and said he'd done 'very, very well out of the pandemic' even though only 0.25 per cent of the masks he sold to the government were ever used amid confusion over the quality of his supplies.

Governments have been overthrown for less.

And that's before we get to Baroness Michelle Mone. She was the Conservative lingerie entrepreneur who leveraged her relationship with Michael Gove to secure a £200m PPE deal – a contract from which her family made a profit of £60m. Soon after she and her husband had pocketed that bounty of taxpayers' cash, she posted a picture of herself standing in a swimsuit on the deck of their newly purchased luxury yacht, the *Lady M*. When reporters, most notably *The Guardian's* David Conn, started asking questions about her involvement in the PPE deal, she told a series of incredible lies, denying she had anything to do with the company that landed the contract. Incidentally, the NHS declared that the gowns she supplied were useless.

We'd already collaborated with the Good Law Project (the organisation which did much to reveal the existence of the VIP lane) by making two films about the wider PPE scandal that we projected onto Parliament and onto the Manchester skyline during the Tory Party conference. But it was Baroness Mone who really interested us. It was her story that we wanted to tell. Not only because of the brazen manner in which she flaunted her pandemic profits, but because the saga spoke to a greater, more pernicious corruption. She'd been given a lifetime seat in parliament and with it the right to vote on the laws that govern our lives, but soon after her ennoblement she'd moved to the

Isle of Man, a tax haven, to live with her husband, who made his fortune by devising tax avoidance schemes. When the couple relieved the British public of £60m in profits in return for apparently unusable PPE, it was to the Isle of Man that the money was spirited.

There was a bigger story to tell here, but it was a complicated one.

We'd previously made a film explaining how Russian oligarchs use London to launder their wealth, and for that we'd deployed an ad van on a tour of the capital (see page 124). Now we wanted to use the same technique to tell the full, mind-spinning story of Michelle Mone and that £200m PPE deal. Our narrator was Dr Meenal Viz, an NHS doctor who'd battled Covid through the PPE shortage. She led us on a tour of Britain, first around Westminster, from the House of Lords to the Cabinet Office to Tory headquarters, explaining how Mone had emailed her Conservative connections to land a place in the VIP lane, despite having no experience sourcing high-grade medical equipment. Then we headed up the M40 towards Heysham Port, where our giant TV boarded a ferry to the Isle of Man.

There we took the viewer to the precise location in which Mone and her husband secreted their PPE profits in an offshore trust, before the screen parked up outside the £25m mansion from where the couple consistently and brazenly lied to the British people (they'd seemingly worked hard to hide the location of their home on publicly accessible documents and we'd spent a day pouring over satellite images to find it).

The final film was, we hoped, the definitive telling of the Mone story and it found an audience of millions. But what we hadn't been able to do was take our TV screen to the *Lady M* – Mone's family yacht purchased soon after she landed the PPE deal. It had last been spotted in that Instagram post somewhere in the Mediterranean, but nobody knew where it was now.

We had a friend whose job it was to find and track oil rigs and tankers, including ones that didn't want to be found and tracked, and we asked him if he could hunt down the *Lady M*. Two weeks later he pinged our WhatsApp group to say he'd traced it to a luxury marina south of Barcelona.

Nothing symbolised the VIP lane like that yacht. It was a £9m floating indictment of a governing party that, in a health crisis, prioritised its friends over frontline doctors and nurses. And it was bought with taxpayers' money that was shelled out for apparently unusable gowns. In fact, we thought, that boat was really *our* boat. It belonged to all of us, and now we'd found it. But what to do with it?

We discussed spiriting it out of that marina and sailing it all the way back to Britain, taking it up the Thames and mooring it at Westminster Pier, then walking the short distance to the Treasury to inform ministers that we'd requisitioned Michelle Mone's yacht for the nation. But we soon concluded we'd likely face charges of piracy and would be unlikely to see our children for some time, so we resolved instead to re-name the boat.

A Spanish friend conducted a stake-out and reported back. There appeared to be a crew onboard the *Lady M*, but they rose late, leaving the boat undefended until about 10am. A nearby security hut was occupied around the clock, but it didn't have line-of-sight to Mone's boat. And crucially, while the *Lady M* and other luxury yachts were in a separate, smaller dock to the other boats in the marina, that dock could be accessed through a channel that was only sporadically patrolled.

This felt like the closest we'd ever get to doing a bank job and still have our families be proud of us. We decided to go for it.

It was a busy time for the project. We were simultaneously running an undercover investigation into MPs' second jobs (see page 176) while planning to paint the road outside the Russian Embassy in London (see page 170). The morning we left for Barcelona, we sent out emails from a fictional South Korean investment firm to 20 MPs asking if they'd like to work for us, then we snapped our laptops closed and left. In our luggage were two huge three-metre-long stickers that we intended to attach to the side of *Lady M*, re-naming Michelle Mone's yacht *Pandemic Profiteer*.

The plan had been to hire the kind of high-powered speedboat that might feature in a mid-70s Bond movie, but it was out of season and we could only find a low-powered launch hired to tourists for day trips that sailed at the speed of a pedalo. Soon after arriving at the marina we took it for a practice run, attempting to apply an imaginary sticker to the harbour wall, but our little boat was so unstable that when one of us stood at the bow the whole thing tipped forward like a giant pudding bowl. Only by each of us sitting in precisely the right spot could one or two of us stand at the front and attempt the re-naming. But it was hard. This was going to be like threading a needle on a rollercoaster.

We retreated to a hotel to plan the next day's raid and to practise applying the giant stickers by fixing them to the wall of the hotel room. The next morning we got up early and headed to the marina to board our boat and attempt the re-naming. With the giant stickers hidden under a picnic blanket we were waved on our way by the kindly owner of our boat, then pootled across the water towards the luxury yachts.

A land team positioned in a café overlooking the yachts radioed to tell us there was nobody on the deck of the *Lady M*. Hearts were beating fast – much faster than the speed of our boat, which was travelling at about four knots. We were 300 metres away. Then 200. Only a few minutes to go now. Then the radio crackled and the café team told us a police launch was now patrolling the marina. A moment later we could see it ourselves. Attempting to look inconspicuous, we sailed past it and then past the luxury yachts and headed out to sea. Only when the police launch moored up did we come back in for another go.

In our experience, if you look like you're meant to be somewhere – that is to say, if you don't act suspiciously – then in general nobody will stop you, even when you're engaged in the most blatant rule-breaking incursion. And so, as we pulled left and slowly chugged through the channel and into the luxury marina, we breezily chatted to each other with the faux-insouciance of a party of millionaires about to rendezvous with our own superyacht.

The *Lady M* was halfway down a row of boats on the right. As we drifted towards it we pulled the stickers out and peeled off the corner backing of the word 'Pandemic'. There was a crew working on the deck of the next boat along but they paid us no attention. We grabbed the anchor line of Mone's boat and pulled ourselves up against the bow to steady ourselves. Then two of us stood at the front of our launch and, as it bobbed heavily, we each planted a hand on the *Lady M*, peeled off the backing and started rolling the material across the surface to apply the huge sticker to the starboard side. But our boat was pitching heavily, meaning it was hard even to stay upright.

'It's wonky,' said one of us from the back of the boat.

'What?'

'The sticker's not straight. Think you need to try again.'

'Seriously?'

By now the crew on the boat next to us had stopped working and were staring down at us. Our sticker definitely wasn't straight, but was it good enough? No. No it wasn't. We hadn't come all this way to achieve something less than aesthetic perfection, so we peeled it back – all the time working hard to keep our balance – then slowly reapplied it, and this time it was straight. Then we took the next sticker, peeled off the backing and stuck the huge sticker to the bow of the *Lady M.*

By now the crew on the yacht next to us was gesticulating to somebody and pointing at us.

'Security's coming!' barked the café crew through the radio as a black launch edged into view from behind the furthest yacht. A man was standing at the wheel and shouting something at us across the water. At the same time another man had appeared above us on the deck of the *Lady M*, holding a cup of coffee and staring at the crew on the adjacent yacht, who were jabbing their fingers at us. He looked down. We were about to pull away and make our escape when we noticed the 'P' of 'Pandemic' had peeled away and a corner of the sticker was hanging limp.

'I think I can reach it!' said one of us, standing at the front of our boat and holding out a toe. But by now we were edging backwards and that toe and our boat were going in divergent directions. Our stickerer grabbed the anchor line and in one movement kicked out to flick the corner of the 'P' against the yacht then fell back into our boat. We turned around and headed for the channel, the security launch in pursuit and the man on the *Lady M* bending over the rails to see what we'd done. The distance between us and the jetty where we'd hired our boat was about 500 metres. We turned the throttle to squeeze every last bit of power from our engine but were still travelling at something only marginally faster than walking speed. The security guy was standing up in his boat and barking into his radio. We sailed out of the channel and turned towards the jetty. It was a furious race for our liberty, at the pace of a stroll to the shops. Four hundred metres to go. He was closing on us, but his boat was pretty slow too. Three hundred metres to go, then 200 metres, then 100 metres. He was right behind us now, calling out in Spanish.

As we pulled up to the jetty the owner of our boat came down the steps, somewhat surprised to see us back so early and with a security guard in pursuit. We jumped out of his boat and onto the jetty, dropped the keys into his palm, told him we'd had a lovely picnic and sprinted towards our van. But when we got there we found the guy from the *Lady M* had parked his car behind our vehicle, blocking us in. He was waving his arms wildly and loudly denouncing us in a South African accent. We all piled into our van, the driver turned the ignition, mounted the kerb and made a pavement exit. And a few minutes later we were on the motorway, heading north for Barcelona.

Michelle Mone's Money

LONDON » ISLE OF MAN

A complex story involving ministers, multiple jurisdictions and millions of pounds. To bring the threads together, NHS doctor Meenal Viz narrated the tale of Mone's millions from the back of an ad van as we toured Westminster and the Isle of Man.

1. (00.05 – 00.34)

My name is Meenal Viz. I'm an NHS doctor. During the first wave of Covid in 2020 I worked in Emergency Medicine in London while I was six months pregnant.

I'm going to tell you a story. It's a story about greed. It's a story about a Conservative peer who used her political connections to make millions of pounds out of useless PPE while nurses and doctors in the NHS struggled on the front line.

2. (00.35 – 01.01)

Our story starts here, at the House of Lords. This is Baroness Michelle Mone of Mayfair. She's a lingerie entrepreneur and a Conservative peer who was given a seat in the Lords by David Cameron. In May 2020 Mone sat down at a computer and wrote an email to Michael Gove offering to source personal protective equipment. At that point Gove was the senior minister here, at the Cabinet Office.

3. (02.00 – 02.33)

By the end of June, the government had contracted to pay £203m of public money to the company Mone vouched for, with an order for 210 million masks and 25 million surgical gowns. By now we'd witnessed the deaths of some of our colleagues and the impact the PPE shortage was having on families across the country. I remember being given one mask for an entire day. It wasn't enough to keep doctors and patients safe.

4. (02.34 – 03.01)

But what about those supplies from Mone's company PPE Medpro? Well, the 25 million surgical gowns for which the government paid £122m were rejected by the Department of Health after technical inspection and were never used in the NHS.

7. (05.20 – 05.45)

A leaked HSBC probe has found that £65m in profits from PPE Medpro were transferred to an entity called The Warren Trust – registered here on the Isle of Man – whose beneficial owner was Barrowman.

5. (03.19 – 03.43)

By autumn 2020, while we struggled to keep the NHS on its feet, Mone had her own challenges. She was planning to marry the financier Douglas Barrowman at the Palace of Westminster, but Covid restrictions forced her to cancel her wedding plans. Instead, she decided to switch the ceremony to the Isle of Man, where there were fewer Covid regulations in place.

8. (05.46 – 06.08)

£46m of that £65m was then transferred to Barrowman's personal account. And a sum of £29m was then transferred from there to The Keristal Trust – registered in this building, again on the Isle of Man – whose beneficiaries were ... Baroness Michelle Mone of Mayfair and her grown-up children.

6. (04.10 – 04.28)

Barrowman owned this sprawling U-shaped nine-bedroom home on the island. And here's what you need to know – because while the couple were making wedding arrangements from here, Barrowman seems to have also been focusing on moving tens of millions of pounds around various Isle of Man registered trusts, companies and accounts.

9. (06.09 – 06.37)

In other words, leaked documents indicate that around the time of her wedding, Baroness Mone and her children secretly received £29m originating from the profits of the PPE business that she pitched to her fellow Conservative parliamentarian Michael Gove – money made in large part from a deal for surgical gowns that turned out to be useless.

Twenty-nine million pounds.

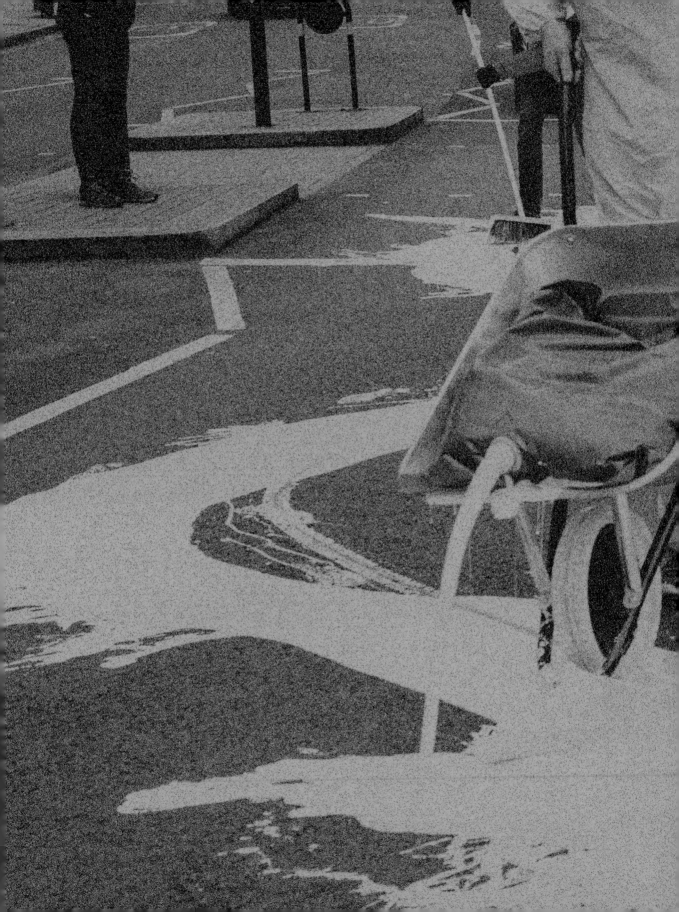

2023

The Lady M

VILANOVA I LA GELTRÚ / SPAIN

Baroness Michelle Mone's yacht was a totemic symbol of the PPE scandal, in which hundreds of millions of pounds of taxpayers' money went to friends of the Conservative Party in return for often unusable medical equipment. Our mission was to re-name Mone's yacht, moored in a luxury marina south of Barcelona.

We used Google Earth to plan the operation, then practised applying the name to a hotel wall before hiring a launch and pulling off the raid (more on this in the essay on page 154).

The Russian Embassy

The idea was simple enough: dump a considerable quantity of red paint in the middle of a busy road and let the traffic do the rest. As cars drove through the paint they'd spread it with their tyres, so soon enough the road would be turned red for hundreds of metres – a river of blood flowing from the Russian Embassy down Bayswater Road in London. A huge visual rebuke to Putin and his imperialist invasion of Ukraine.

Up to now, many of the giant displays of support for Kyiv had been delivered by governments. Lighting up the Eiffel Tower, projections in Downing Street, that kind of thing. We wanted to do something that was quite obviously the work of the public, something that no government PR department would ever sanction. Confrontational. Grassroots but epic.

But would commuters drive through our paint? And how would we dump it in the road without causing a pileup?

Sitting in the Café Diana opposite the embassy, observing Russian security details and the frequency of diplomatic police patrols, we discussed potential methods of paint delivery. Intermediate bulk containers (IBCs) hold 1,000 litres of liquid and are used to deliver and distribute water in a humanitarian crisis. We considered sticking one of those on the back of a flatbed truck, parking the thing in the road and turning the tap. But at a flow rate of 30 litres a minute (we googled it) the police would shut us down before we'd created so much as a puddle.

With an array of framed photographs of the late Princess of Wales looking down on us from the café walls, we then discussed the merits of sourcing a kids' paddling pool, inflating it, filling it with paint, putting *that* on the back of a truck and slashing it with a knife as we pulled up outside the embassy to release the paint.

Even Diana looked dubious.

Buckets, bicycle panniers, balloons …

we went through a host of delivery options, even considering buying a fire engine and spraying the paint from a hose (there was one on eBay). Then our friend Veronica – who was leading on logistics – suggested we use wheelbarrows. Keep it simple, she said. Keep it safe. And she was right.

But how many barrows did we need? And how much paint? We wanted the road to be red across the facade of the embassy, so about 200 metres in total, but in both directions. Shot from a helicopter that would look amazing. We crunched through some calculations and decided 250 litres should do it. Call it 320 litres to be safe. Four wheelbarrows, 80 litres of paint in each, two on the eastbound carriageway, two on the west, each team with someone to stop the traffic and someone to brush the paint out, making it safe to drive through.

By now it was a fortnight before the first anniversary of the invasion, when we wanted to do this thing. We found a non-toxic, chalk-based paint that would ping with colour but safely wash away and were about to order it when we were struck with sudden and severe second thoughts. The four of us jumped onto Zoom.

A river of blood? Could that be construed as a bit angry? Our objective was to show people in Ukraine and around the world that it wasn't just governments opposing Putin's colonial misadventure. But was a blood river inspiring, or might it come across as a bit, well, deranged?

Our Zoom conversations are free-ranging affairs that easily jump from family updates to raging denunciations of the state of national and global affairs to creased-up bouts of collective laughter to creative breakthroughs. On this particular call it was suggested that we could fill the westbound wheelbarrows with yellow paint and the eastbound ones with blue paint to create the world's biggest Ukrainian flag outside Putin's embassy. We mocked it up on a photo, decided immediately that it spoke to hope and would be a powerful rinse of the

Russian dictator, and altered our order of paint. We also decided not to use a helicopter, believing we'd get the shot from a cherry-picker (the kind of vehicle used to fix telephone cables) and brought the day of deployment forward by 24 hours so our picture would be in the newspapers on the morning of the anniversary.

But hang on … if cars pulled out of side roads and drove through the yellow paint then down the blue side of the road, would we succeed only in creating a green road and thus a massive *Libyan* flag? We bought two tins of paint – blue and yellow – and headed out to a quiet patch of tarmac in the countryside for some real-world testing. The colours didn't easily mix (good news) but the paint didn't easily wash off the tyres of our test vehicle (not so good). We pondered setting up a soap-and-bucket tyre cleaning station on Bayswater Road but decided instead that we'd carry a handful of £20 notes on the day to hand out to any irate drivers whose wheels needed a professional spray.

Two weeks later 15 of us gathered in a car park next to the embassy at 9am, beside a cherry-picker and a van containing wheelbarrows and four huge bladders of paint. The previous day had been spent mixing the stuff in the LBD warehouse and now we were ready to launch what we'd codenamed 'Valspar'. We'd recruited some friends to help us and by 9.15am we were lifting the paint bladders into the wheelbarrows. The yellow team set off down the road to their lay-up point in a side street near the eastern corner of the embassy, while the blue team waited at the entrance to the car park on the western corner. The four of us plugged in earphones and jumped into a WhatsApp audio chat, then the paint tippers pulled on blue or yellow paper suits and we were ready to go.

'Okay all?'

'Yup, ready.'

'Yellow team about to go. Unscrewing lids now.'

'Lids off here too, blue team also ready to … *Argh wait!*'

The blue team was standing on the pavement dressed in their blue suits with their blue paint spilling from their wheelbarrows, while 30 metres away, strolling towards them, were two Metropolitan police officers.

'Cops.'

'Shit.'

'Go anyway?'

'Go go go!'

At the eastern and western corners of the embassy we stepped out into the road and stopped the traffic, holding signs that read 'UKRAINE SOLIDARITY PROTEST – DRIVE SLOWLY – WASHABLE PAINT'. A moment later we tipped the wheelbarrows and paint poured onto the road, and a moment after that the blue team was set upon by the police. The blues tried breezily chatting to the officers while still pouring paint, but the cops determinedly wrestled them away from the wheelbarrows and dragged them to the pavement.

Meanwhile, the unimpeded yellow team disgorged their paint across the westbound carriageway in a great geyser of colour. They tried to brush it out but there was just too much of it. A lake of paint now sat undisturbed on one side of the road. A van driver was screaming at us through his window, car horns filled the air, the police were radioing for back-up, the traffic wasn't moving and even if it did then our flag would only be yellow. Those of us still at large were waving at the drivers to brave the paint but nobody moved. Failure and humiliation loomed. We needed one person, just one, to go first, then others would follow. That's how crowds work. But the traffic was frozen.

After perhaps two minutes, during which time it felt like the whole Led By Donkeys project hung in the balance, one car edged forward. Its tyres rolled through the paint, came through the other side and left two long streaks of colour down the road beyond. Then another car came forward, and another, and then a bus. We watched with relief as the traffic flowed and a broad yellow stripe started stretching down the street.

But what about the other side? The blue team was by now being handcuffed, but we could still speak to each other through our earpieces.

'Someone needs to get the blue paint out,' whispered one of the arrestees. 'Get the paint out.

'Hey, who are you speaking to?' barked a cop.

In a flash one of the yellow team darted over the road, pulled the two blue bladders from the overturned wheelbarrows and dragged them along the tarmac, leaving a trail of paint behind him. The traffic followed and a streak of blue started to form. High above our heads a photographer in the cherry-picker recorded the scene as cars crawled through the two pools of paint and a Ukrainian flag emerged slowly on Bayswater Road in front of the Russian Embassy.

But had we bought enough paint? The blue team (comprising half of LBD and two friends) were loaded into a police van, and as they were driven to Charing Cross Police Station they stared out of the back window for minute after minute at more than a mile of yellow road.

Yes, we'd bought more than enough paint. And we should have hired that helicopter.

As one of our friends thrust a £20 note through the window of a black cab (not everyone was impressed by our efforts) the yellow team stripped out of their paper suits and headed incognito to a nearby hotel. We needed to collate the footage we'd shot and make a film of the intervention. The room was on the sixth floor and from there the unending extent of blue and yellow could be viewed in both directions, as far as the eye could see. More importantly, in front of the embassy the colours met with stark luminescence and the road was now a big, bright, brilliant flag.

As soon as the video was edited and posted to our social media accounts, the yellow team headed to the police station to wait for the blues to be freed. It was a long wait, but after 15 hours they were released into the night. They hadn't seen any of the coverage so were relieved to hear that our flag had already featured on TV news bulletins across the globe.

'The police told me I had a right to make a phone call,' said one of the blue team. 'After I saw how far the paint had spread I thought about calling the helicopter company. But I couldn't remember the number.'

Painting the Flag

The paint for this intervention at the Russian Embassy was mixed in the Led By Donkeys warehouse – a task that was only finished late on the evening before deployment. The next morning we gathered in a car park around the corner from the embassy, then pushed the wheelbarrows into position. We had expected some resistance from drivers, but it was a routine police patrol that proved to be a greater challenge.

It was around midnight when we were all released. By then, the picture of our flag had gone around the world.

MPs For Hire

WESTMINSTER, LONDON / UK
SEOUL / SOUTH KOREA

During a cost of living crisis, we wondered, when people needed their MPs more than ever, would a serving Member of Parliament consider taking a job furthering the interests of a foreign company on top of their constituency duties? And if so, how much would they want to be paid? The answers, it turned out, were 'yes' and 'a lot'.

Working with legendary investigative reporter Antony Barnett, we set up a fake South Korean investment company and emailed 20 MPs from all parties, asking if they'd be prepared to join our international advisory board. The role, we said, would require a day a month of their time but remuneration would be competitive.

FREE MAGAZINE INSIDE

20 best Sunday lunch recipes

Old favourites and new surprises from Nigel Slater, Nigella Lawson and more

In the New Review

Succession's hall of shame Famous fans pick favourite scenes

In the magazine

Recipe for disaster
Is an AI chatbot a better food critic than Jay Rayner?

The Observer

www.observer.co.uk | Sunday 26 March 2023 | £3.50

From £3.03 for subscribers

Former Tory chancellor Kwasi Kwarteng and former health secretary Matt Hancock were fooled into attending online meetings for a fake South Korean firm. Led by Donkeys

Top Tory MPs ask for £10,000 a day to work for fake company

- Kwarteng, Hancock duped by campaigners
- Video released of talks over pay rates

Jon Ungoed-Thomas

The former chancellor, Kwasi Kwarteng, and former health secretary, Matt Hancock, agreed to work for £10,000 a day to further the interests of a fake South Korean firm after apparently being duped by the campaign group Led by Donkeys. Kwarteng attended a preliminary meeting at his parliamentary office and agreed in principle to be paid the daily rate after saying he did not require a "king's ransom". When Hancock was asked his daily rate, he responded: "It's 10,000 sterling."

Sir Graham Brady, the chair of the 1922 committee, also attended an online meeting for the fake foreign firm from his parliamentary office. When asked about the limits on arranging meetings, he made clear he could not advocate on behalf of the innocent but said he may be able to advise the firm on who to approach in government. He said a rate of about £6,000 a day "feels about right" and any payments would be on a public register.

A fourth MP, former minister Stephen Hammond, who had been approached, said this weekend he considered he had been the victim of a "scam". He said he thought he was engaged in a preliminary discussion with a company but "it turns out this company was fake, with a fake website". Hancock's spokesperson said he had acted "entirely properly".

The senior politicians have complied with all relevant rules and referred to their obligation to their constituents during preliminary meetings. The Led by Donkeys pro-

Continued on page 9 >>

Stress from Ofsted investigations linked in coroner reports to 10 teachers' deaths

Anna Fazackerley

Stress caused by Ofsted inspections was cited in coroners' reports on the deaths of 10 teachers over the past 25 years, the Observer can reveal.

The research, by charity the Hazards Campaign and the University of Leeds, will intensify what Ofsted has called the "outpouring of anger" in the sector over the death of Berkshire headteacher Ruth Perry, who killed herself in January. Her family have attributed her death to the inspectorate having downgraded her school.

Education unions called last week for all inspections to be halted.

It comes as an Observer investigation has found that the pressure of school inspections has led to headteachers suffering heart attacks, strokes and nervous breakdowns, and as a helpline for heads reports that the vast majority of crisis calls it receives are now about Ofsted.

Andrew Morrish, a former head and founder of Headrest, a resource for stressed headteachers, said that after being told by inspectors that their schools were being downgraded or graded inadequate, heads had "felt school in an ambulance", suffering panic attacks, heart attacks or strokes brought on by stress.

Carol Woodward, award-winning

Continued on page 13 >>

DID YOU REMEMBER?
Clocks went forward by an hour last night

Undercover Reporter:

Do you have a daily rate at the moment?

Matt Hancock:

I do. I do, yes. It's 10,000 sterling.

Five MPs agreed to be interviewed by us, including Matt Hancock, Kwasi Kwarteng and Sir Graham Brady. Soon they were sitting in secretly recorded Zoom meetings, candidly discussing their careers with our Vice-President for External Affairs at her corporate HQ (in reality a Korean reporter sitting by a window in an Airbnb, the Seoul skyline over her shoulder).

It was just six months since Kwarteng, as Chancellor, had crashed the UK economy with his disastrous mini-budget. Nevertheless, he offered us an unflinching account of his talents before agreeing a fee of £10,000 for his one day a month, even giving himself a pay rise mid-exchange as he shifted from dollars to pounds. Hancock also rated himself at £10,000 a day and £1,500 an hour, while Sir Graham pitched himself at £60,000 for his 12 days a year.

Nice work if you can get it (they didn't, at least not with us).

Farage's Failure

MULTIPLE LOCATIONS / UK

Farage got there in the end. In an interview with BBC *Newsnight* he admitted 'Brexit has failed'. But with most newspapers adopting an *omerta* on Brexit scepticism, we crowdfunded for a national advertising campaign to highlight Farage's concession. Our posters went up across the country.

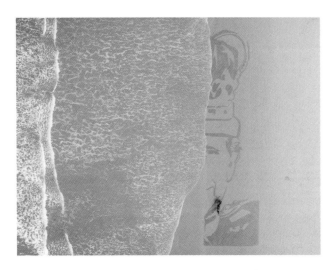

The Coronation

REDCAR, NORTH YORKSHIRE / UK

When Charles III ascended the throne among
the kind of pomp and ceremony that is typically the
preserve of those who are never elected by their
peers, we knew we wanted to say something. Rather
than the sledgehammer approach of calling for an end
to monarchy in a country where royalty still receives
significant support, we wanted to leave people with a
question that they might ponder while they watched the
coronation ceremonies – could, should, this king be
the last? Our film of the installation ended with a poll
that found less than one-third of young people thought
the monarchy should continue.

Thames Water HQ

READING, BERKSHIRE / UK

To the list of perilous pursuits engaged in by Britons in the 2020s (trying to get a GP appointment, putting the heating on, protesting government policy etc.) we can now add the once relatively risk-free act of going for a swim in the sea. When Thames Water revealed it was in financial trouble and might seek a taxpayer bailout, we produced a film detailing how, since being privatised, Britain's water companies had accrued £60bn of debt while paying out £57bn in dividends to their shareholders, often based abroad, leaving too little for investment in the infrastructure that would protect our rivers and beaches. Both metaphorically and actually, water privatisation has been a shitshow. The film was projected onto the Thames Water HQ.

Labour Headquarters

How to fix a huge spoof campaign banner to the Labour Party headquarters without getting stopped?

Keir Starmer had made a host of promises to Labour members when he campaigned for the leadership in 2020, many of which he subsequently jettisoned. We'd dug up a quote from the campaign about electoral reform and mocked up the kind of unmissable advertising awning that Labour might have rolled out if the party wasn't now running away from Starmer's words.

Hanging it on the party's London headquarters required one of us to act as a distraction by playing the role of an officious delivery agent who claimed that the banner had been ordered by the marketing department. As he approached the security booth and tapped at his clipboard, demanding a

signature, the rest of us scaled the scaffolding and fixed the awning in place.

Our current voting system – first past the post – is profoundly unfair and needs to change, favouring as it does the two main parties and rendering millions of votes next to worthless. A fairer and more proportional system would make every vote count. It could, if done well, help to breathe new life into our politics and encourage greater participation.

First past the post works so well for our two main parties that they're both reluctant to change it. Never more so than when they have power, or think they're about to get it. That's why we decided to visit Labour's Head Office to remind Keir Starmer of his words in support of proportional

representation when he was campaigning to become leader of the Labour Party.

The overwhelming majority of Labour members (83 per cent when last polled in 2021) support proportional representation and want the party to deliver this change. We're not starry-eyed about proportional representation. It's not without risks and challenges. Nor is changing the voting system a silver bullet. Our democracy, like many around the world, is seriously degraded and under threat. We fail to nurture and regenerate it at our peril. As the last few years have shown, democracy is not a natural endpoint of the evolution of human political systems, it is an idea and it needs to be fought for.

As well as reforming the electoral system, there is a huge amount that could be done to rejuvenate British democracy. For example, lowering the voting age to 16, abolishing the Lords and replacing

it with a second elected chamber based in a northern city, using citizens' assemblies to guide and steer local and national decision-making and introducing a written constitution to better enshrine citizens' rights and rules for our political leaders.

No matter who is in power, we are committed to fighting for the kind of ambitious, meaningful change that would renew our democracy. We can't take for granted that any government of any stripe will make these changes without us all stepping up as citizens to demand them.

Some observers were surprised to see us deliver an intervention directed at Labour in opposition. But it's always been core business for Led By Donkeys to confront politicians with their own words when they become less convenient. This is an accountability project and that doesn't change even when the party in power does.

"... millions of people vote in safe seats and they feel their voice doesn't count. That's got to be addressed by electoral reform."

Sir Keir Starmer, February 2020

🌹Labour

Rupert Murdoch

NEW YORK CITY / USA

Few people have done more damage to Britain than media magnate Rupert Murdoch. Long before his company hacked the phone of a murdered teenager, he was exploiting his power to dictate government policy and influence election outcomes.

Having reached millions with biopics of Johnson, Farage and Rees-Mogg, we made a film detailing the billionaire's serial atrocities against decency and democracy. The film was narrated by J. Smith-Cameron, star of the TV show *Succession*, which is loosely based on the Murdoch family. She joined us for the shoot as we projected the biopic onto the New York skyline.

Glastonbury

PILTON, SOMERSET / UK

With the NHS under ever-greater pressure after years
of inadequate funding and still reeling from the impacts of
the pandemic, we teamed up with the Glastonbury Festival
to send a message of support and appreciation for the UK's
most loved institution. We chose the word 'stand' to try to
reflect some of the energy of the tens-of-thousands
of revellers who stand and jump to their favourite bands
performing on the iconic Pyramid Stage.

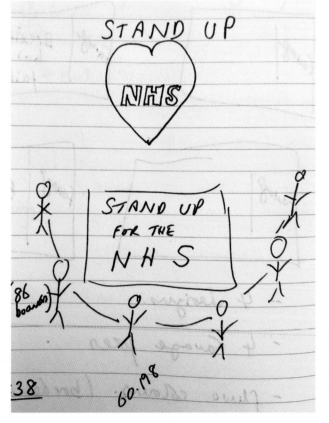

TAND THE

HS

it was quite an entertaining kidnap

Yes, it might have happened, but so what?

Rwanda Scheme Exposed

MAYFAIR, LONDON / UK

The government's plan to deter migrants from crossing the Channel was to engage in performative cruelty by sending some of them to Rwanda. Ministers claimed the African country was safe for refugees. Experts disagreed. We went undercover to expose the truth.

Working with reporter Antony Barnett, we created a fake Malaysian investment company and asked Rwanda's sometime PR guru, London-based Terence Fane-Saunders, if we could meet him to discuss potential investments in Rwanda. We also expressed a desire to meet UK ambassador and former Rwandan Justice Minister Johnston Busingye. The following month, our operative was sitting opposite the men at an exclusive Pall Mall club, wearing a hidden camera.

Fane-Saunders told us Rwanda had kidnapped former opposition leader Paul Rusesabagina (he described the abduction as 'entertaining'), while Busingye discussed the killing of at least 12 refugees by Rwandan police in 2018, saying: 'Yes, it might have happened, but so what?'

Our investigation was cited numerous times in parliament as MPs and Lords debated the Rwanda legislation. Our follow-up investigation revealed that Britain was granting asylum to Rwandan refugees – a position at odds with ministers' claims that the country was safe.

Stop the Sleighs / Nasty Party

MATTHEW PARKER STREET, LONDON / UK

 Christmas time / Mistletoe and wine / Children singing Christian rhyme / With logs on the fire and gifts on the tree / It's time to construct an overhead Christmas lights deck and hang it over the front of the ruling party's headquarters before flashing satirical festive messages and Tory policy failures at the building.

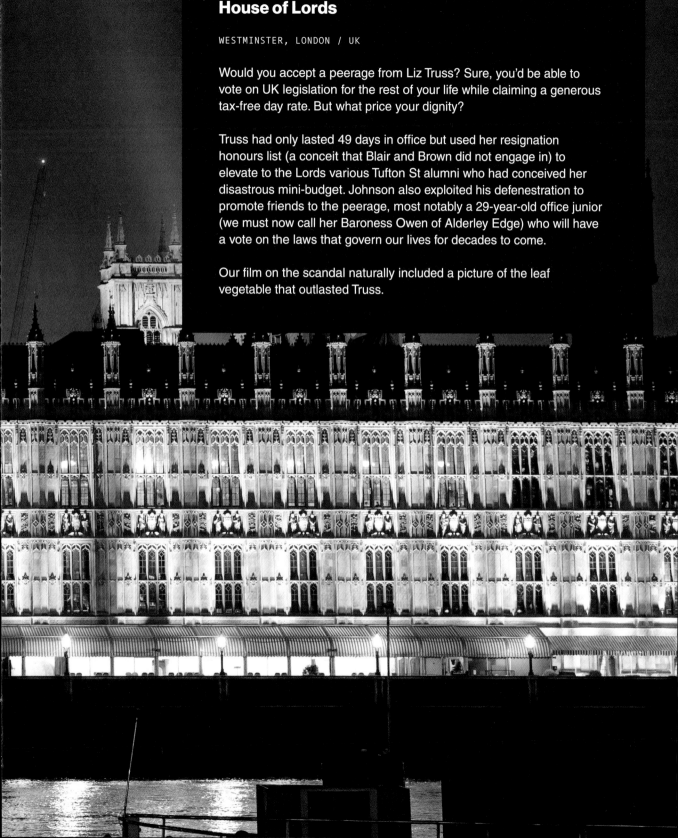

House of Lords

WESTMINSTER, LONDON / UK

Would you accept a peerage from Liz Truss? Sure, you'd be able to vote on UK legislation for the rest of your life while claiming a generous tax-free day rate. But what price your dignity?

Truss had only lasted 49 days in office but used her resignation honours list (a conceit that Blair and Brown did not engage in) to elevate to the Lords various Tufton St alumni who had conceived her disastrous mini-budget. Johnson also exploited his defenestration to promote friends to the peerage, most notably a 29-year-old office junior (we must now call her Baroness Owen of Alderley Edge) who will have a vote on the laws that govern our lives for decades to come.

Our film on the scandal naturally included a picture of the leaf vegetable that outlasted Truss.

Gaza

Often we create films that are a barrage of information, cramming in as many facts, quotes and damning bits of evidence as we can into a widely-shared piece of content. But sometimes we're trying to do the opposite, we're trying to communicate one single thing, a hard-to-comprehend fact that needs a deeper treatment. The kind of fact that butts up against some limitation in our brains to understand what something really means. And for that we're looking to translate that fact into something you can experience in a different way.

The fact we wanted people to grasp was the number of children killed in Gaza. It had long become incomprehensible. What the UN would call a 'graveyard for children' was witnessing a Palestinian child killed every ten minutes. At the end of October 2023, just three weeks into the war, Save The Children put out a statement saying the number of kids killed had surpassed the total from all conflicts worldwide in the previous four years.

By January 2024, when we resolved to deliver an intervention, the toll of children killed in Gaza had more than tripled and was approaching 11,500. We decided from the outset we wanted to include in any intervention the 36 Israeli children killed on 7 October. Not because of a false equivalence between the death tolls but because no child should die in war and all should be mourned.

We wanted to cut through the perceived complexity of the conflict. More than 99 per cent of children who'd been killed had died at the hands of the Israeli military. What is often characterised as a conflict between two sides is beginning, rightly, to be understood as the occupation and oppression of one people by another.

Our idea was to show what it would feel like to walk past all those kids. A line of 11,500 children, stretching 6 kilometres in length.

But made of what? We considered a chalk outline of children, printed by a giant roller at the front of a truck. Could we drive it from Hyde Park Corner to the Israeli Embassy in the middle of the night? It felt too jokey, and besides, we didn't think we'd be able to pull it off. Then came the concept of thousands of funeral shrouds, to echo the pictures of mass burials that were flooding social media. But that felt heavy and morbid.

The breakthrough idea was using secondhand kids' clothes. Could we lay 11,500 sets out on a beach somewhere? We got some from a charity shop and one of us headed home to pair up tops and bottoms and set them out. Even laying out just five outfits felt devastating. We had a concept.

Now we just had to source over 20,000 items and get them ready to lay out, and all in less than two weeks. Diving into the world of secondhand clothes wholesalers, within a few days five tonnes of mixed kids' clothes had been delivered to our London warehouse.

By this time we'd settled on a date a little under ten days away that looked pretty dry on the south coast. A call for volunteers went out – dozens responded and booked the day off work. We were committed now.

The main challenge was the sorting and pairing of clothes. It's no good having a baby grow matched with a 12-year-old's tracksuit bottoms. With an immovable deadline looming, volunteers were working full-tilt in the warehouse, but there was no predicting when the emotion of what this all represented would break a helper's focus. Often it was while looking down at an item of kids clothing with something like 'best brother' scrawled on it. After a sit down or a hug, people got back to it.

All this time we were still looking for a location. We needed somewhere we could access that wouldn't immediately get shut down but that was also public enough to be experienced, and long enough to fit 11,500 sets of children's clothing placed side by side. Having rejected Brighton Beach (not long enough) and Camber Sands

(tide line too high), just three days before our date we drove down to recce Bournemouth Beach. It was just right.

Another wrinkle: the weather. Even in summer a British beach is a bit of a gamble. In February it's closer to guaranteed rain and we knew that the chances of our dry window staying that way was slim. If the weather was wet we'd struggle to lay out the clothes and critically we wouldn't be able to fly the drone to show the clothes close-up – a key part of the concept with no obvious solution.

Sometimes when an action starts you just know it's going to work. This was *not* one of those times. As we arrived at the beach at first light, we couldn't even see the pier clearly from the start point through the haze. It felt impossible.

But we had to try. We drew a 6km guide line in the sand using a weight attached to a rope. Then two big vans of clothes arrived, and then the coach from London, with fewer people than we'd hoped. But local volunteers started coming down to balance the numbers. An initial rain shower cleared and people started following the deployment plan developed by our friend Rob, who was leading on the logistics.

Our initial aim was to install at least one complete section that we could capture, even if the authorities stopped us from continuing. But soon after, a councillor arrived and gave us their personal thumbs-up. We knew then that we were unlikely to be stopped by the police and that our only remaining hurdle was the scale of the task. We needed more people. We put up call outs on social media and local radio.

By now, nearly 100 volunteers were working tirelessly to lay down thousands upon thousands of tops and bottoms, pushing through the cold and the constant paralysing reminder of what these clothes represented. Halfway through it still looked like an impossible task. We considered trying to film the line the next morning if we had to finish installation in the darkness. But the incoming bad weather might jeopardise that. We already had a helicopter booked for 2pm, to capture images out of

reach of any drone. We pushed it to 3pm and everyone kept going without breaks.

By the time the helicopter was heading out from the airfield, something had shifted. Bolstered by local recruits and the collective determination for this not to fall at the final hurdle, the installation was accelerating. The line was now over 5km long and approaching the final stretch after the pier. In half an hour it would be finished, just at the moment the helicopter would be flying into position.

Back at the other end of the beach, more than 6km away, the drone pilot was fighting heavy headwinds in the fading light to capture the start of the film. By the time darkness fell we had a bunch of shots from the helicopter and the drone, but no idea whether we had something that worked. We headed to a room we'd booked in the Premier Inn as an edit suite.

It was a strange feeling. We'd completed the installation. We'd laid out a 6.5km line of 11,500 children's clothes. We'd done media interviews on the beach, and many Bournemouth residents had turned up to walk at least part of the line. We knew it had moved everyone who'd seen it but our ambition was for it to resonate with people around the world and we still didn't know if we had good enough pictures.

It was a nervy few minutes as we flicked through the footage. From the drone there was one take (from dozens) that realised our vision of a slow bird's-eye start where you could connect with each child and then accelerate and tilt at a bewildering speed to cover about half the line. It was the same with the helicopter footage. The conditions meant that most of it was unusable, but the final shot matched up seamlessly.

Twenty minutes later, we had a final edit. After a last play through, the room was silent for a long time. By the following day, many millions of people had watched the film. We hoped we had created and captured something that gave meaning to that incomprehensible number, something that took people closer to understanding the scale of what was happening in Gaza.

The Beach

BOURNEMOUTH, DORSET / UK

The effort to lay out more than 20,000 items of children's clothing in a line more than 6km long in the space of a few hours required a meticulous plan. It also relied on the support of dozens of volunteers.

Resupply

- Stock teams 1–4 at Rockwater Car Park, Branksome Chine.
- Teams 7 & 8 will do the transportation.
- Send Sky's car with supplies for Teams 5 & 6 to Alum. Chine Car Park & Durley Chine Harvester Car Park.
- Send Team 7 to help transport from the car to Teams 5 & 6 on the beach.
- Once nearing completion of 3km, make sure 7 has all 20 bags at start and move all vans to Bournemouth Pier Car Park to continue supply.
- Teams 1 & 2 relieve Teams 7 & 8.
- Some car access to Underhill Drive east of Bournemouth Pier.

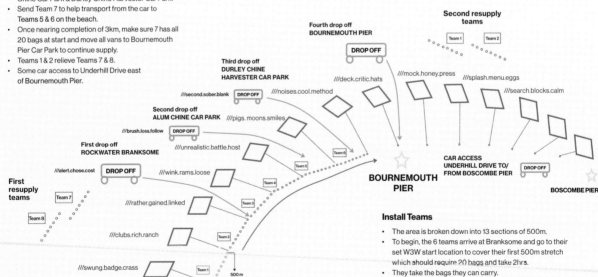

Second resupply teams

Team 1   Team 2

Fourth drop off
BOURNEMOUTH PIER

DROP OFF

///mock.honey.press   ///splash.menu.eggs
///deck.critic.hats   ///search.blocks.calm

Third drop off
DURLEY CHINE HARVESTER CAR PARK

///noises.cool.method

///second.sober.blank   DROP OFF

Second drop off
ALUM CHINE CAR PARK   ///pigs. moons.smiles

///brush.loss.follow   DROP OFF

///unrealistic.battle.host

First drop off
ROCKWATER BRANKSOME

Team 6

///alert.chose.cost   DROP OFF

Team 5

First resupply teams   ///wink.rams.loose   Team 4

Team 7

///rather.gained.linked   Team 3

Team 8

///clubs.rich.ranch   Team 2

///swung.badge.crass   Team 1

500 m

BOURNEMOUTH PIER

CAR ACCESS
UNDERHILL DRIVE TO/
FROM BOSCOMBE PIER   DROP OFF

BOSCOMBE PIER

Install Teams

- The area is broken down into 13 sections of 500m.
- To begin, the 6 teams arrive at Branksome and go to their set W3W start location to cover their first 500m stretch which should require 20 bags and take 2hrs.
- They take the bags they can carry.
- Once a team is finished with a section, they move EASTWARDS, to help the next team.
- Once Team 6 is finished, all teams move onto the next stretch finishing the final 2.75 km around Bournemouth Pier together.

It would take more than two books full of pages like this to show the entire length of the line. The picture on the following page represents less than two per cent of the installation.

Thumbs Up to Extremism

BRISTOL / UK

Rishi Sunak's press office let it be known he was about to make an important speech about extremism from the steps of Number 10. Was he about to address the zealotry that had engulfed his own party, including the support by leading Conservative figures for the man who had attempted to subvert American democracy? No, he was not. Instead, he confined his comments largely to a critique of supposed left-wing fanaticism.

We mobilised to remind people that some extremists held real power in Britain.

Not only did he arrest me, he also shook my hand and said I'm proud of you

The Bibby Stockholm

PORTLAND, DORSET / UK

We rebranded the barge housing refugees, then projected the testimony of Rafi Hottak, an interpreter for the British Army in Afghanistan who was injured in a Taliban attack. Rafi was forced to flee his homeland before making it to the UK across the Channel.

Speaking in our film about the people held on the barge, Rafi asked the government, 'Have you even listened to them? Have you heard their stories?' As we packed up to leave, the police arrived. Two weeks later, Sunak called an election.

Extremists.

Led By Donkeys

Acknowledgements

Deepest thanks to Fionn Guilfoyle, Veronica Pasteur, Emma Fry, Graeme Furley, Sam Keyte, Antony Barnett, Gavin Esler, Alice Russell, Fionn McSherry, David Hirst, Saf Suleyman, Kevin Nugent and Anna Nolan who have made an invaluable contribution to this project.

Special thanks as well to David Allen Green, Carol Armistead, Colin Armistead, Claire Ashforth, Elika Aspinall, Samantha Batt-Rawden, Alun Bethell, Alex Boyle, Oliver Bullough, Sadie Butler, Rob Callender, Richard Chitty, Daphne Christelis, Clara Collingwood, Aisle 3 in Bethnal Green Co-op, Tim Cowen, Ali Deacon, Charlie Denholm, Nick Dewey, Said Durra, Emily Eavis, Brian Eno, Elly Farmer, Paul Finn, Graham Forbes, Anna Ford, Matt Fowler, Joss Garman, Lizzie Gilson, David Godwin, Jo Goodman, Marie Jacquemin, Carla Grande, Guy Guerrini, Zarlasht Halaimzai, Fran Hall, Kate Harrison, Ben Hayes, Anna Hedges, Marina Hyde, Armando Iannucci, Claire Jamieson, Farrah Jarral, Matt Knifton, Julia Knowles, Sam Knowles, Laura Marchant, Aram Martirossian, Ahmed Masoud, Luke Massey, Jolyon Maugham, Jed Mercurio, Gavin Millar, David Mirzeoff, Dan Mokades, Elena Morresi, Chris Morris, Nathan Oswin, Laura Parker, Liz Pendleton, Mark Philipp, Elahe Pope, Leyla Pope, Martin Pope, Chris Ratcliffe, Jo Rendle, Kate Rodde, Alex Rose, Colin Rose, Irene Rose, Steve Russell, David Schneider, Paul Sherlock, J. Smith-Cameron, Steve Smith, Patsy Stevenson, Jan Stewart, Marie Stewart, Mark Stewart, Mishelle Stewart, Richard Stewart, Tricia Stewart, Paul Stupple, Rachel Taylor, Jack Taylor Gotch, Hagop Tchaparian, Graham Thompson, Eloise Todd, Tabitha Troughton, Roxana Vilk, Peter Vilk, Joshua Virasami, Meenal Viz, Carol Vorderman, Jamie Wardley, Liz Webster, Monica Wyer and Shimri Zamaret.

Thank you to everyone else who has contributed to Led By Donkeys projects in any way – there are simply too many to mention here.

And most importantly, thank you to our partners and children who have put up with so much. Without their love and support none of this would have been possible: Tabs, Rosa, Kit, Arvid, Isaac, Lorna, Scout, Willow, Emily, Elsie and Belle.

Photo Credits

pp.2–3, 30–31, 33, 34–35, 38–39, 50, 51, 56, 57, 58–59, 60, 61, 66, 67, 68–69, 74, 108, 120, 132, 33, 191 (bottom right), 192–93 © POW. pp.4, 42, 157, 159 (pics 5, 6, 9), 163 (top right), 194 (bottom right), 197 (top left, bottom), 212–13 © Saf Suleyman. pp.7, 50, 51, 60, 78, 79, 109, 110, 114, 116–17, 121, 123, 124, 126, 127, 144, 158, 159 (pics 7, 8), 164–65, 168, 190, 191 (top right, bottom left), 207 (top left, top right), 208 (top right, bottom left), 219 © Fionn Guilfoyle. pp.16 (bottom left), 17 (top right) © Jack Taylor Gotch. p.21 © Joe Hunter. pp.22–23, 60, 61 © Jiri Rezac. pp.28–29, 61, 180 (first row, middle, third row right, fourth row right), 180 (bottom) © Jeremy Sutton-Hibbert. p.40 © Phil Fearnley – Halo Vue Aerial Filming. p.43 © Panoptic Motion. pp.44, 45, 195 (second row left) © Sand In Your Eye. pp.48–49 © Arena Aviation. pp.52, 62 (top left), 104–5 © Luke MacGregor. pp.54–55 Colin McPherson. pp.63 (top), 64–65, 68–69, 70–71, 80–81, 91 (bottom right), 92 (first row left, first row middle, first row right, second row right, third row left, fourth row right, fifth row right) 93 (top, bottom), 96 (second row left), 103, 105, 112–113, 119, 122, 143, 145, 146–47, 148–49, 152, 153, 181 (top), 184–85 © David Mirzeoff. pp.72–73, 90 (top), 91 (top), 92 (second row left, third row middle, right, fourth row left, middle, fifth row left, middle), 96 (top row left, right), 160–61, 171 (bottom), 172, 173, 174–75, 188–189, 200–201, 202–203 © Chris J Ratcliffe. p.94 (second row middle) © Richard Gray. pp.76, 77 © Hassan Akkad. pp.94–95 © Leon Neal/Getty Images. p.96 (second row right) © Matthew Chattle/Future Publishing/Getty Images. p.97 (top right) Sky News. pp.98–101 © Adam Butler. p.107 (top) © Nathan Stirk/Getty Images. pp.106 (bottom left), 150, 180 (second row middle, fourth row left, fifth row middle) © Mark Harvey. pp.107 (bottom), 118, 138–39, 180 (first row right, third row middle) © Dean Atkins. pp.115, 116–117 © BBC. pp.128–29 © Brian Smith. pp.134–37, 210 © Flying TV. pp.140, 141 © Sununu Hernandez. p.151 © Peter Nicholls – Pool/Getty Images. p.180 (first row left, second row left, second row right, third row left, fourth row middle, fifth row right) © Jon Super. pp.182, 183 © Paul Everett/Xcytemedia. pp.196–97 © Matt Cardy. pp.204–205, 218 © Ollie Harrop. p.210 (bottom) © Alice Russell.

All other photos © Led By Donkeys.

**Led By Donkeys is 100% funded
by small donations.**

We refuse major donors.

**If you'd like to become a
supporter please scan the code.**

or visit donate.ledbydonkeys.org

First published in the United Kingdom in 2024 by
Thames & Hudson Ltd, 181A High Holborn, London WC1V 7QX

Reprinted 2024

Designed by Steve Russell / aka-designaholic.com

British Library Cataloguing-in-Publication Data
A catalogue record for this book is available from the British Library

ISBN 978-0-500-29812-1

Printed in Bosnia and Herzegovina by GPS Group

Be the first to know about our new releases,
exclusive content and author events by visiting
thamesandhudson.com
thamesandhudsonusa.com
thamesandhudson.com.au

Led By Donkeys